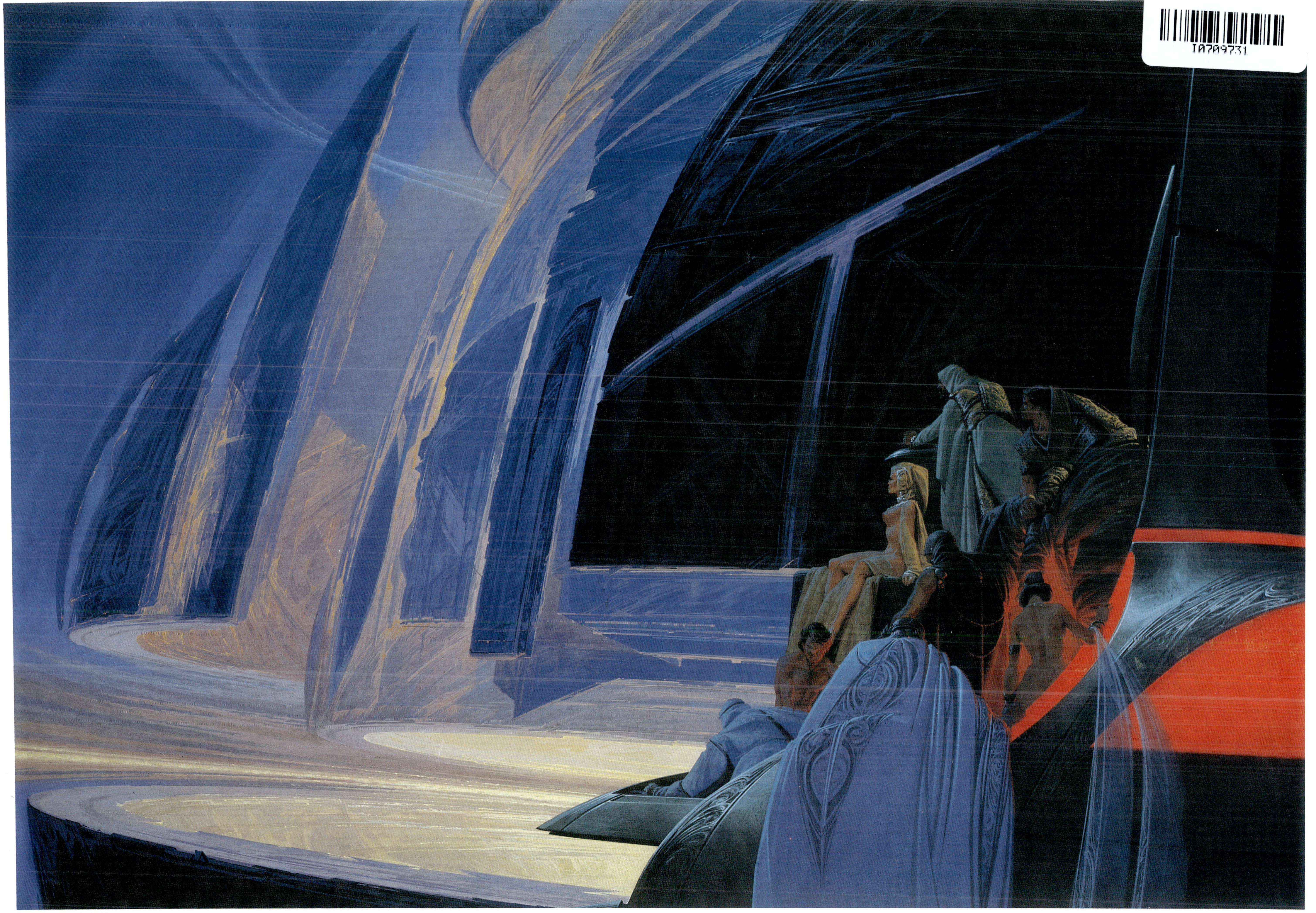

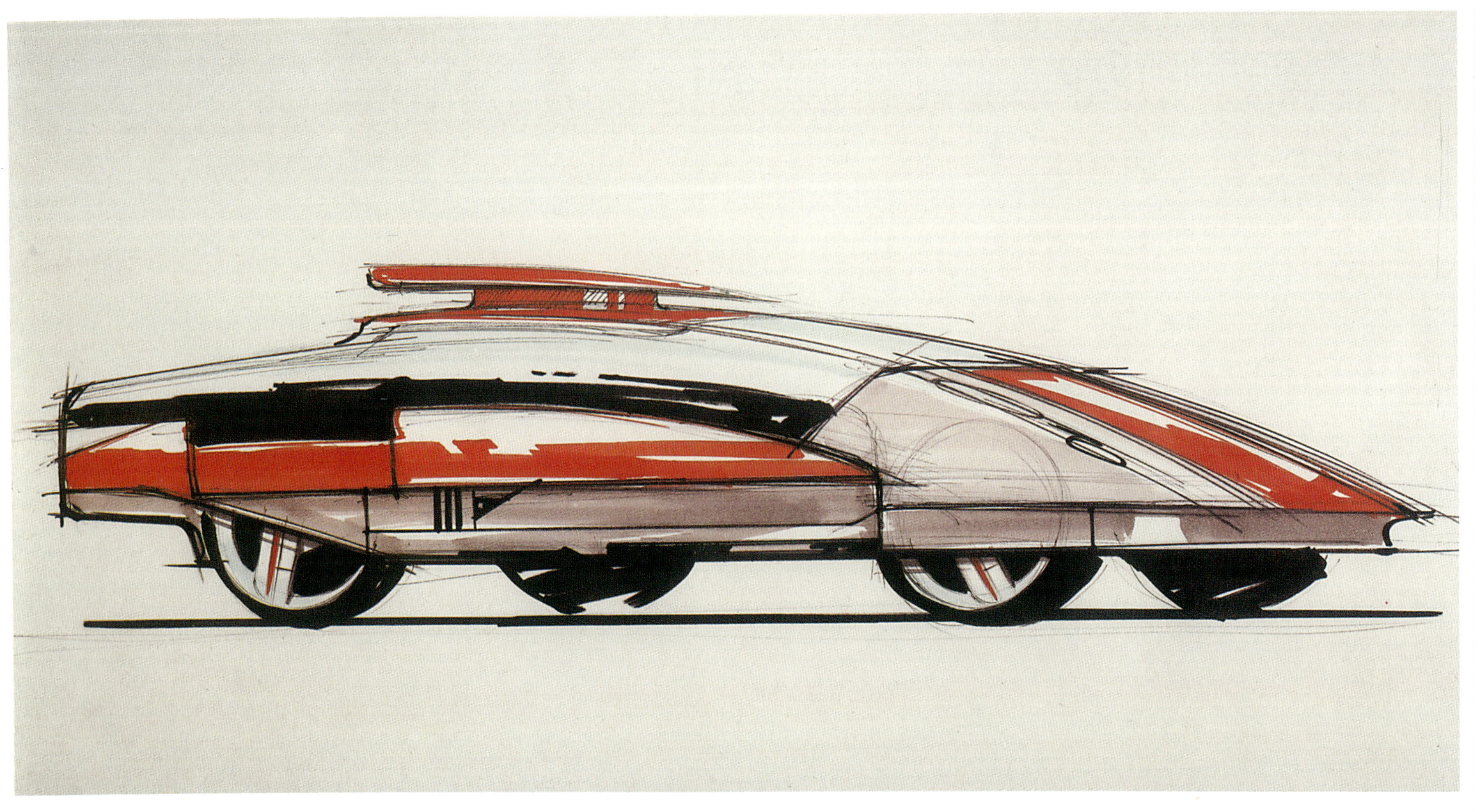

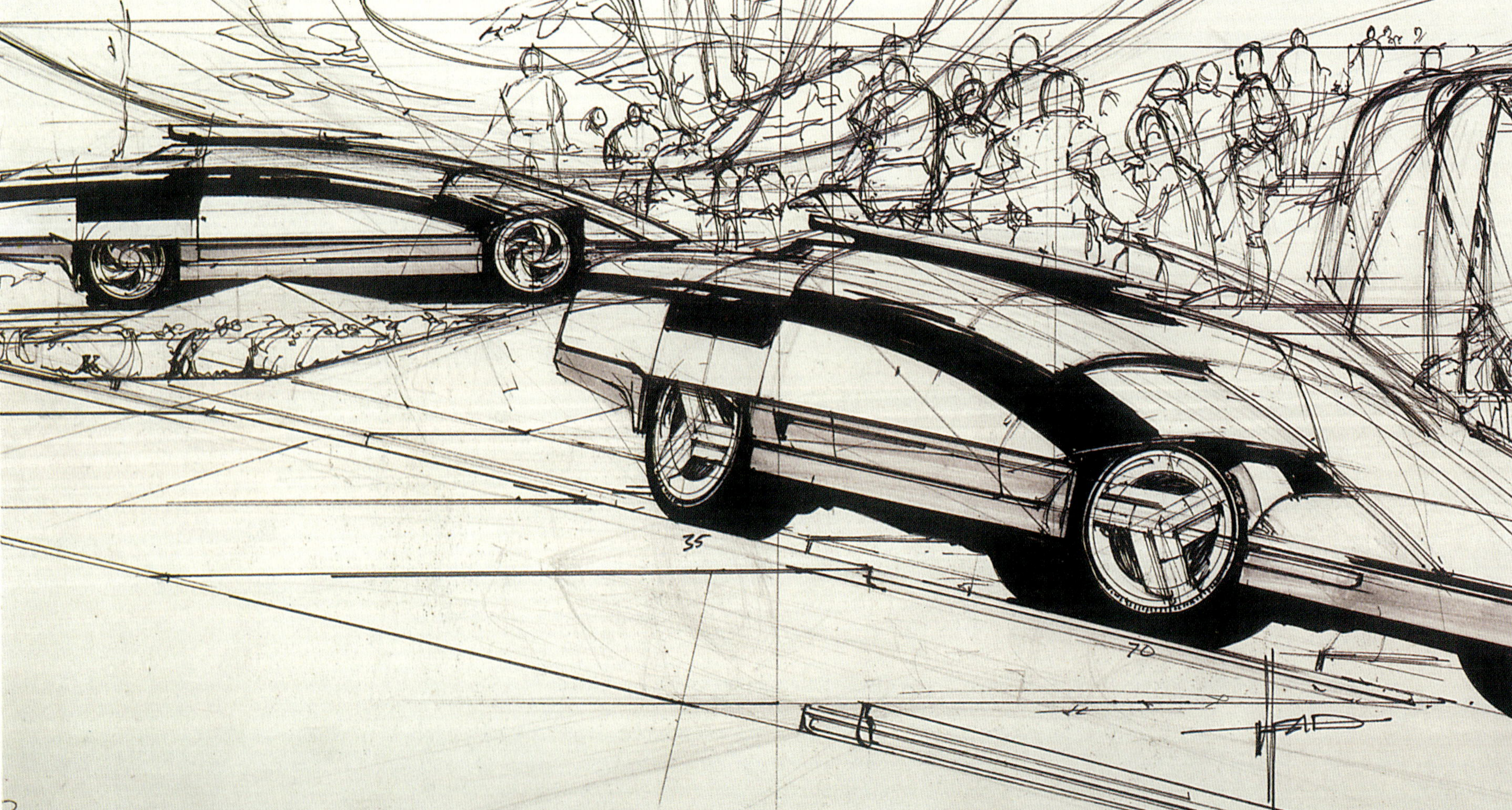

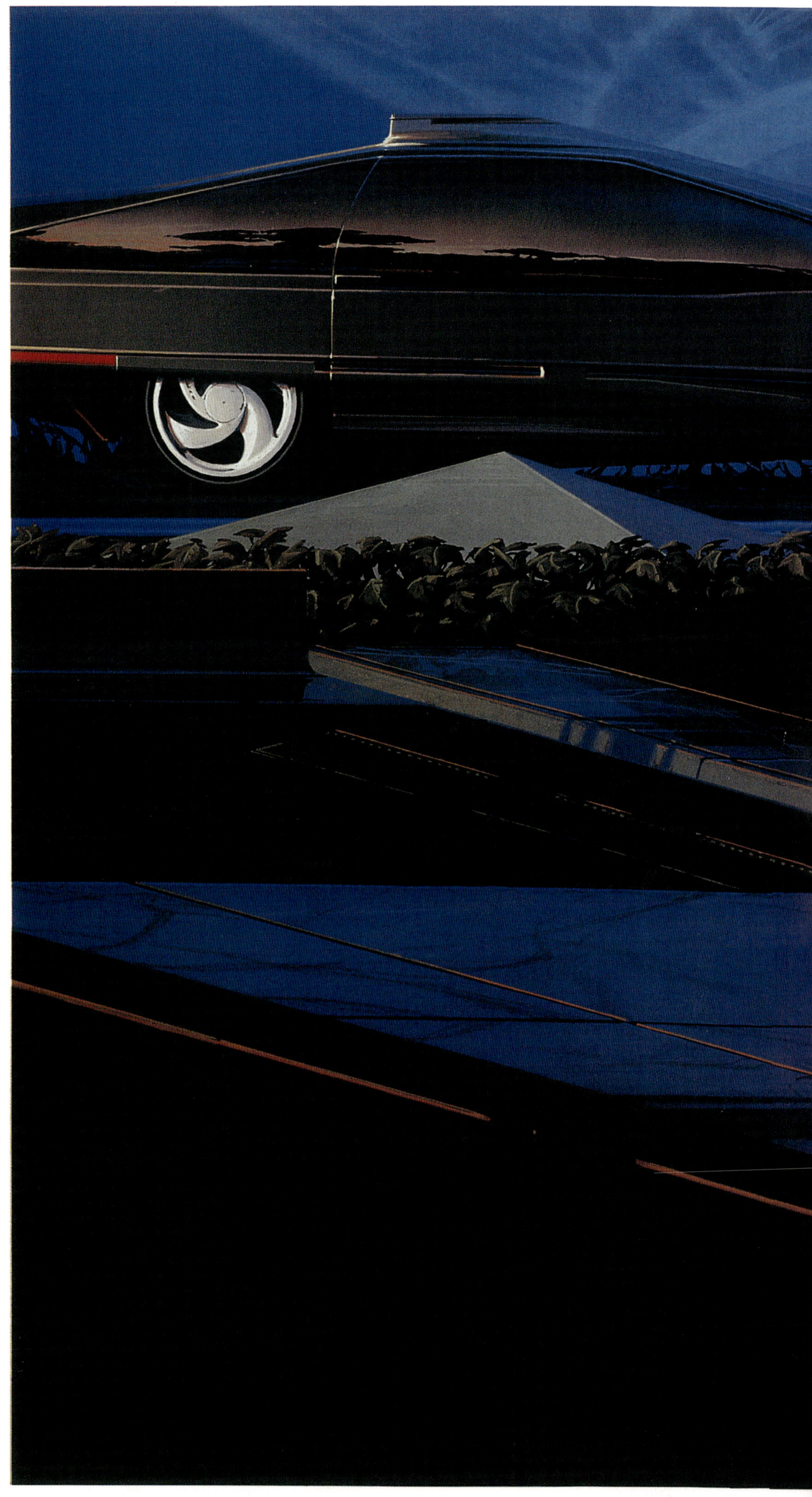

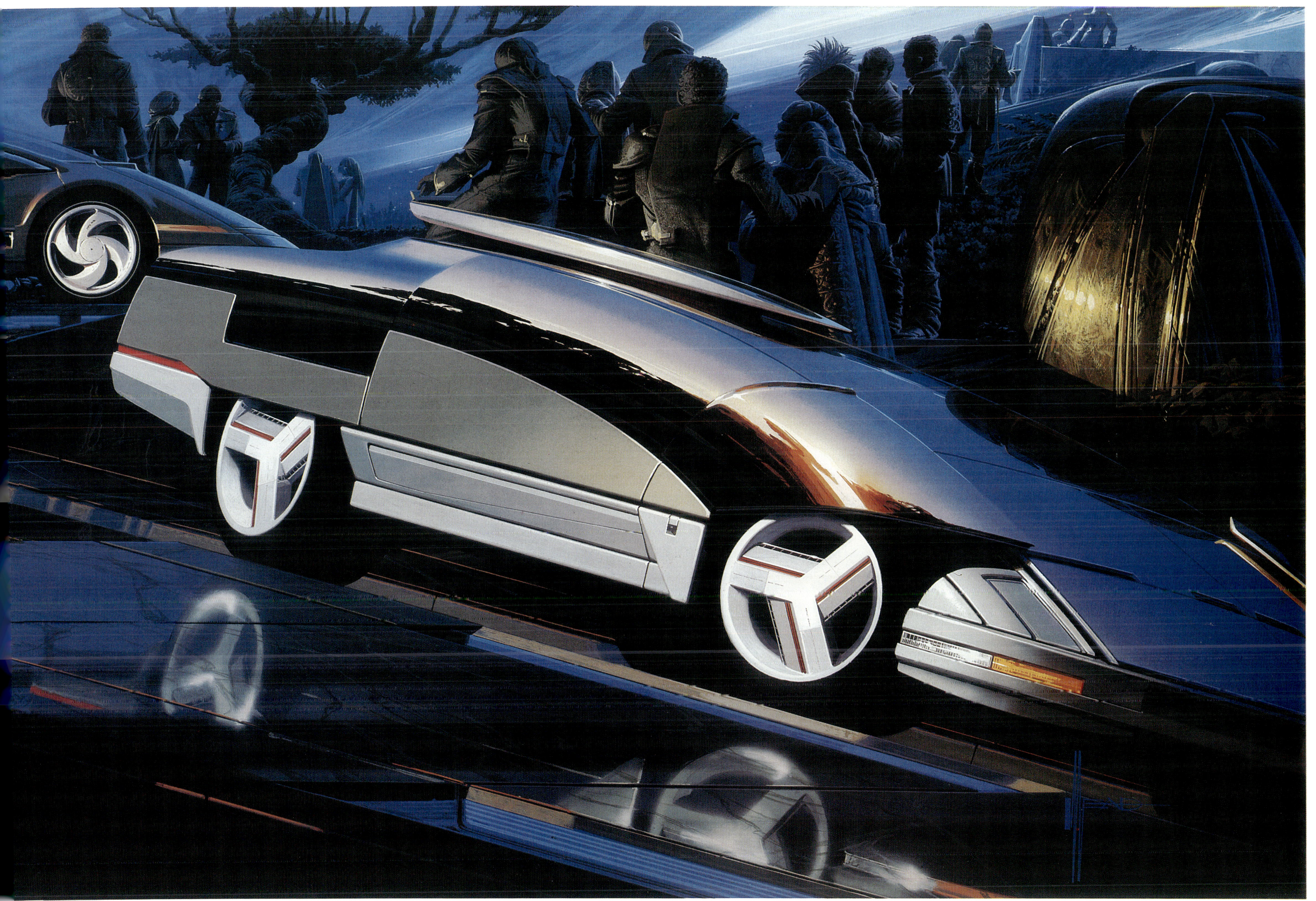

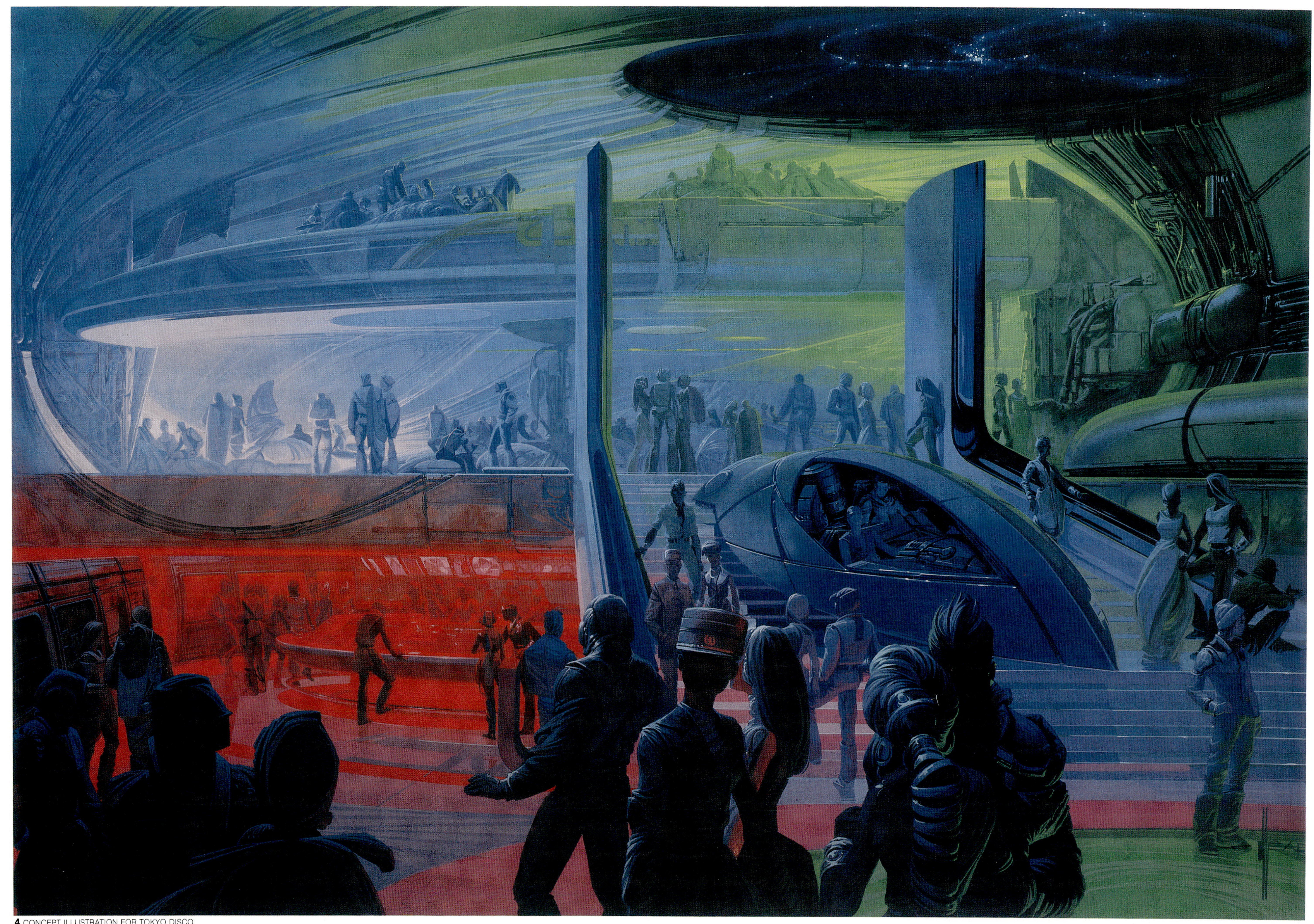

4 CONCEPT ILLUSTRATION FOR TOKYO DISCO

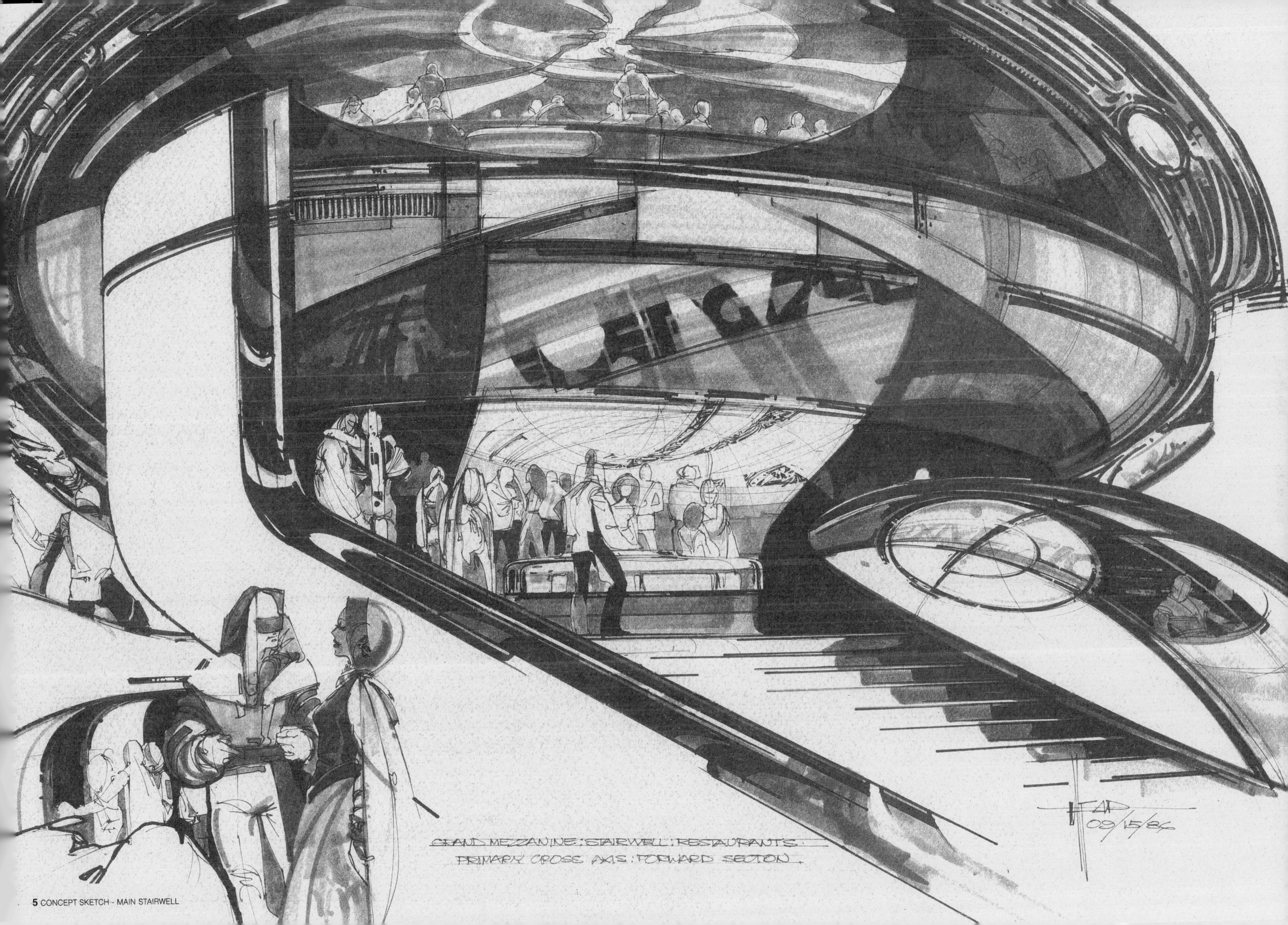

GRAND MEZZANINE : STAIRWELL : RESTAURANTS :
PRIMARY CROSS AXIS : FORWARD SECTION

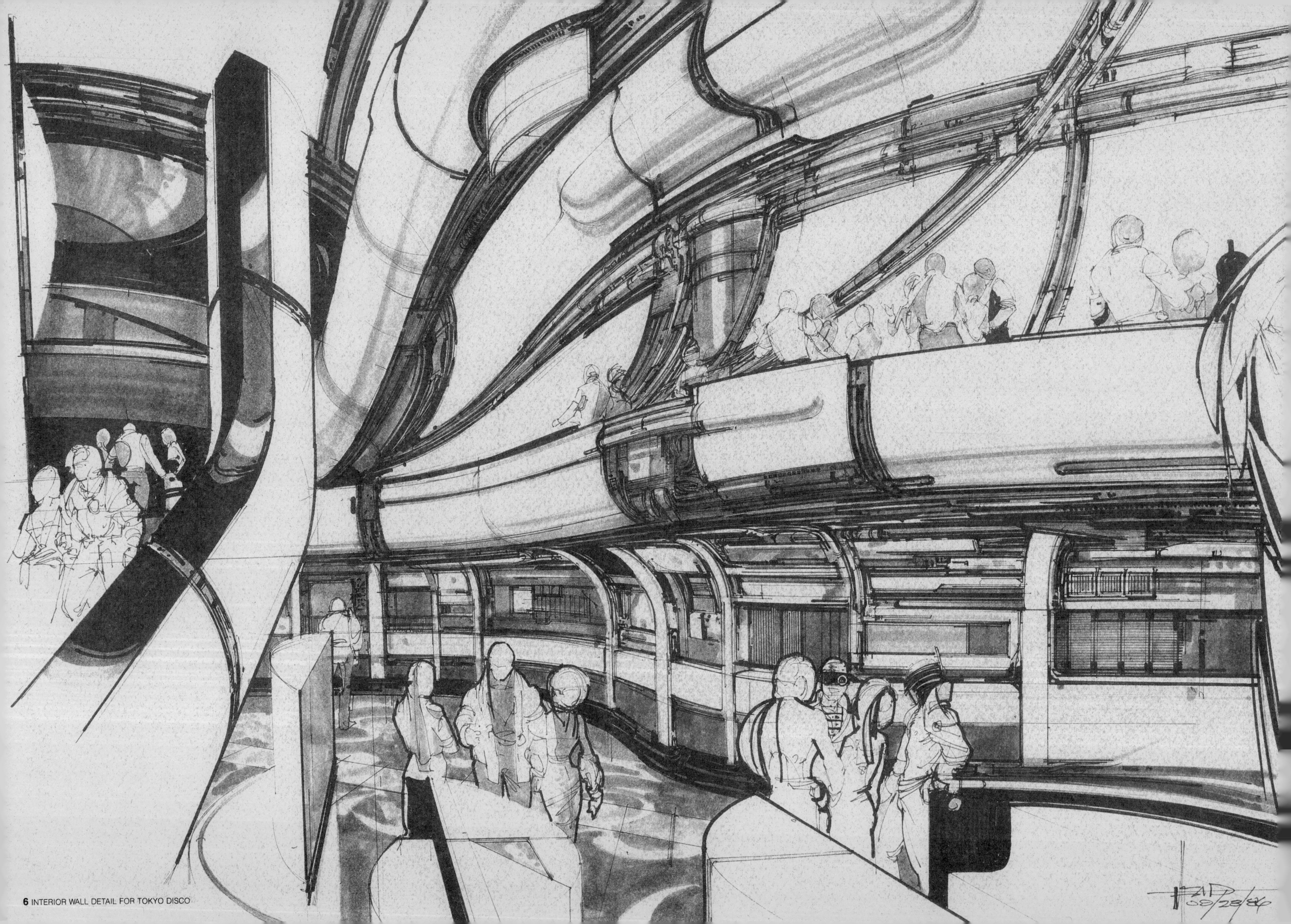

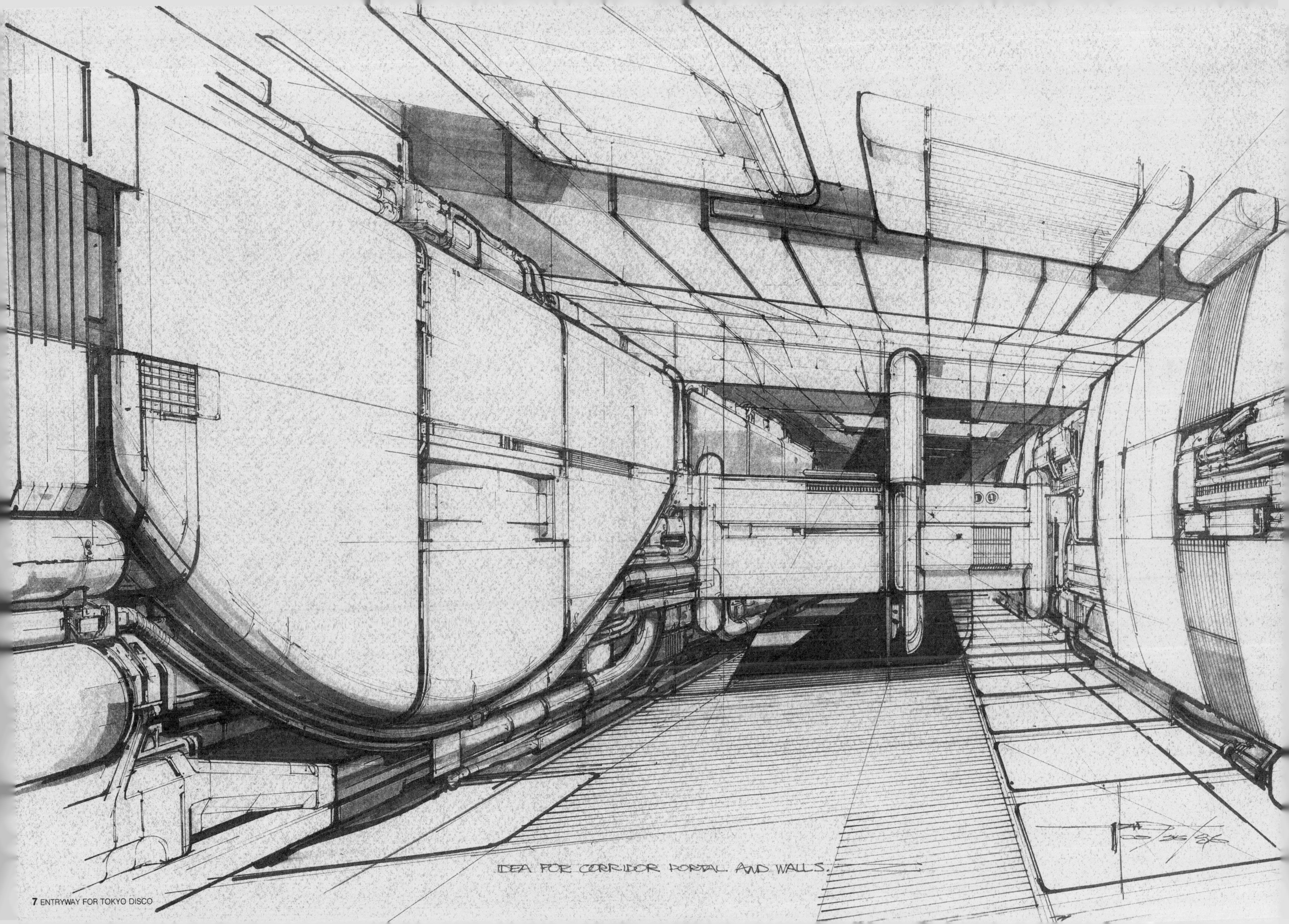

IDEA FOR CORRIDOR PORTAL AND WALLS

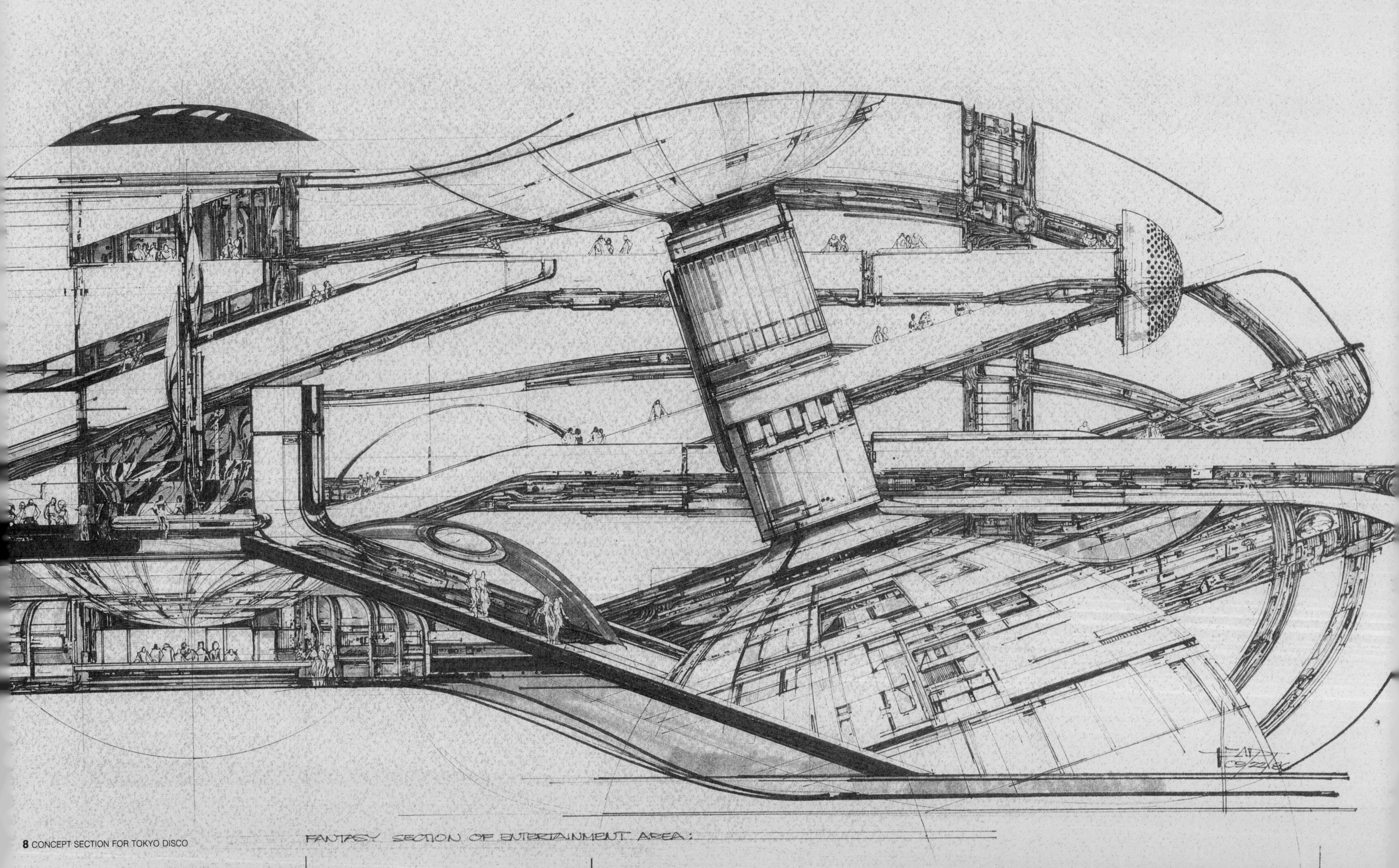

FANTASY SECTION OF ENTERTAINMENT AREA.

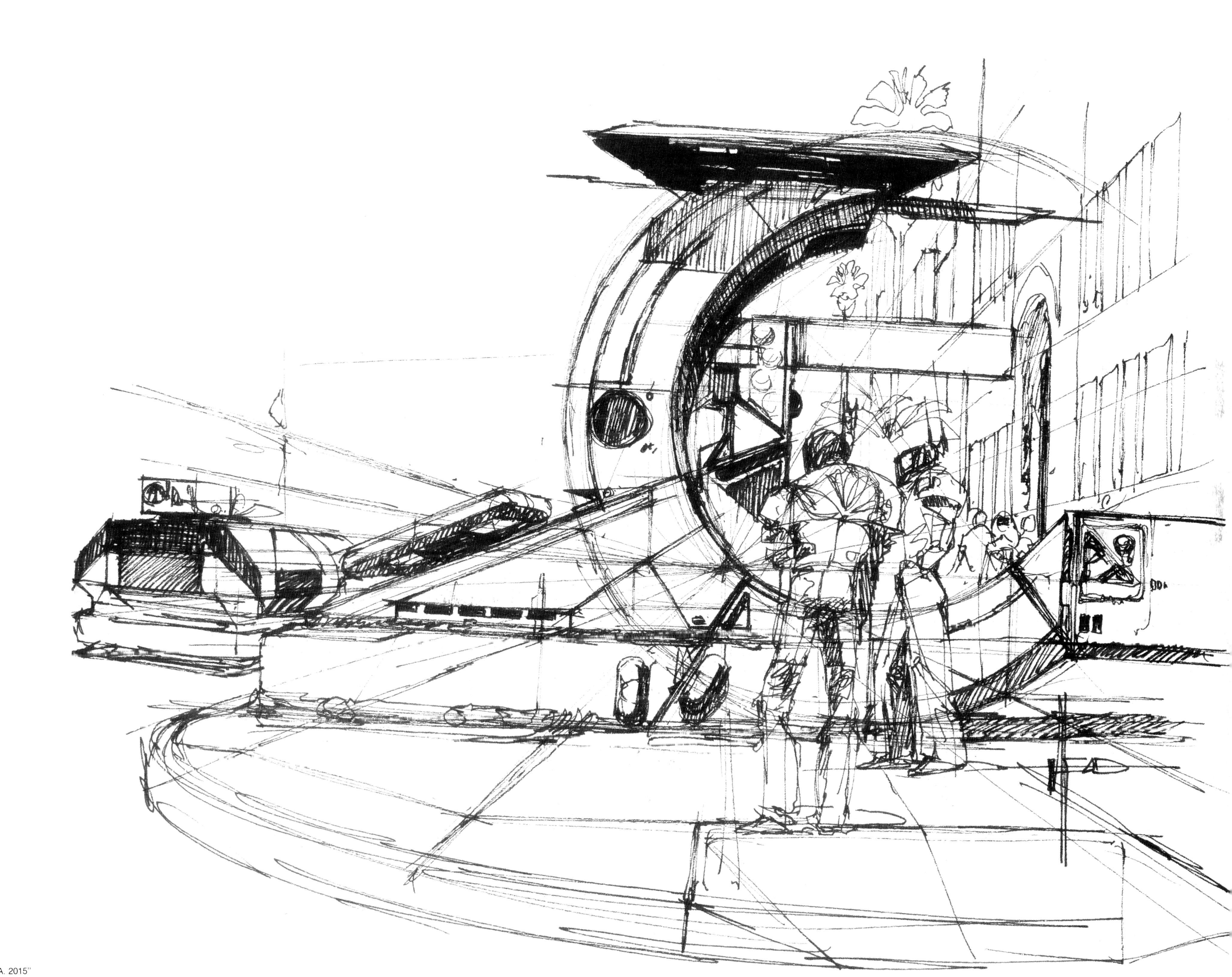

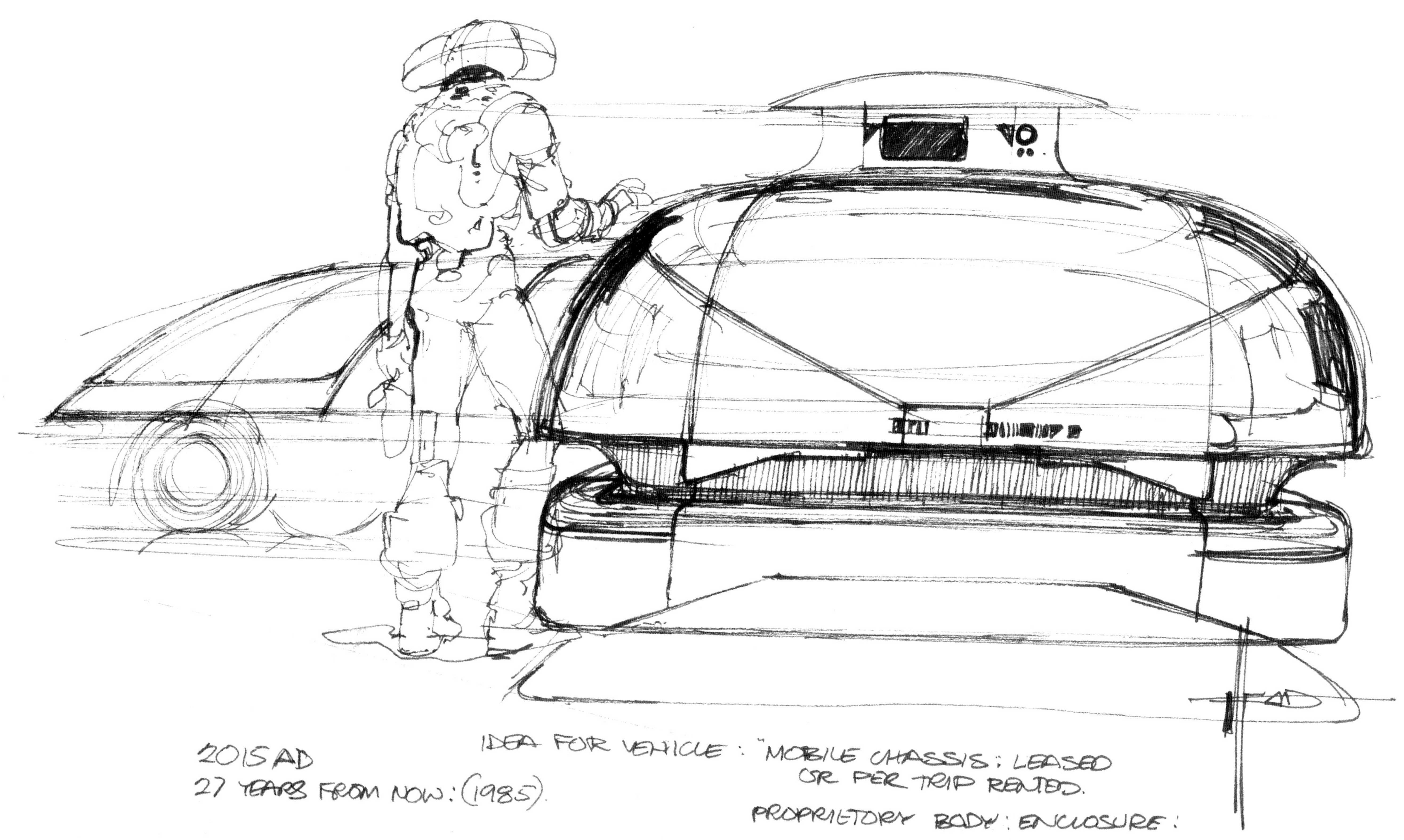

2015 AD
27 YEARS FROM NOW: (1985).
IDEA FOR VEHICLE: "MOBILE CHASSIS: LEASED
OR PER TRIP RENTED.
PROPRIETORY BODY: ENCLOSURE:

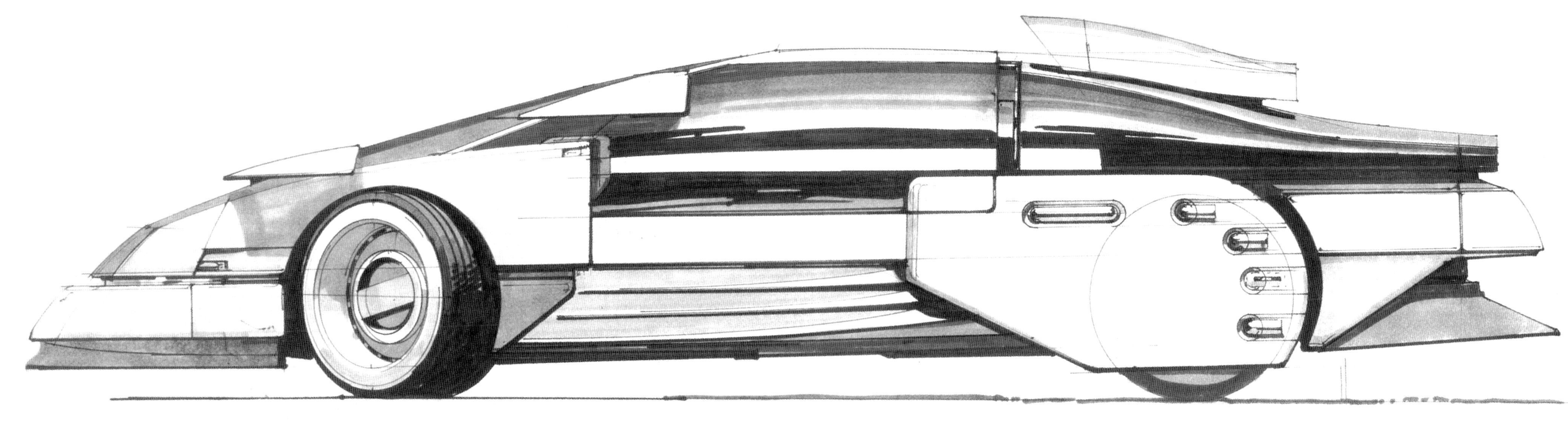

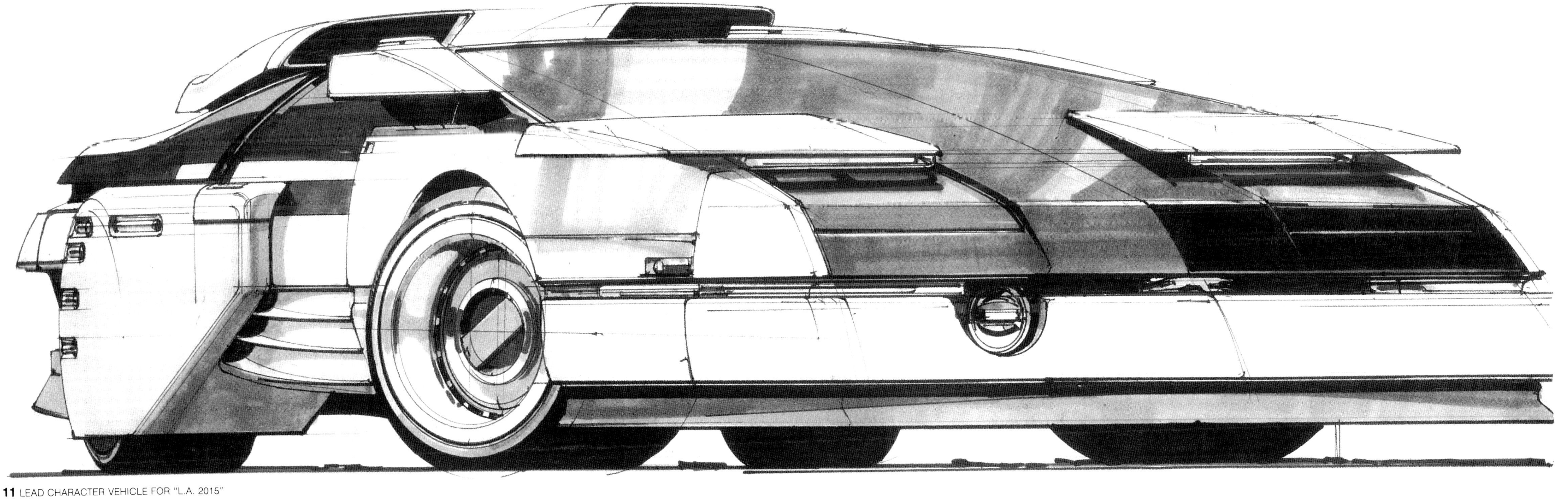

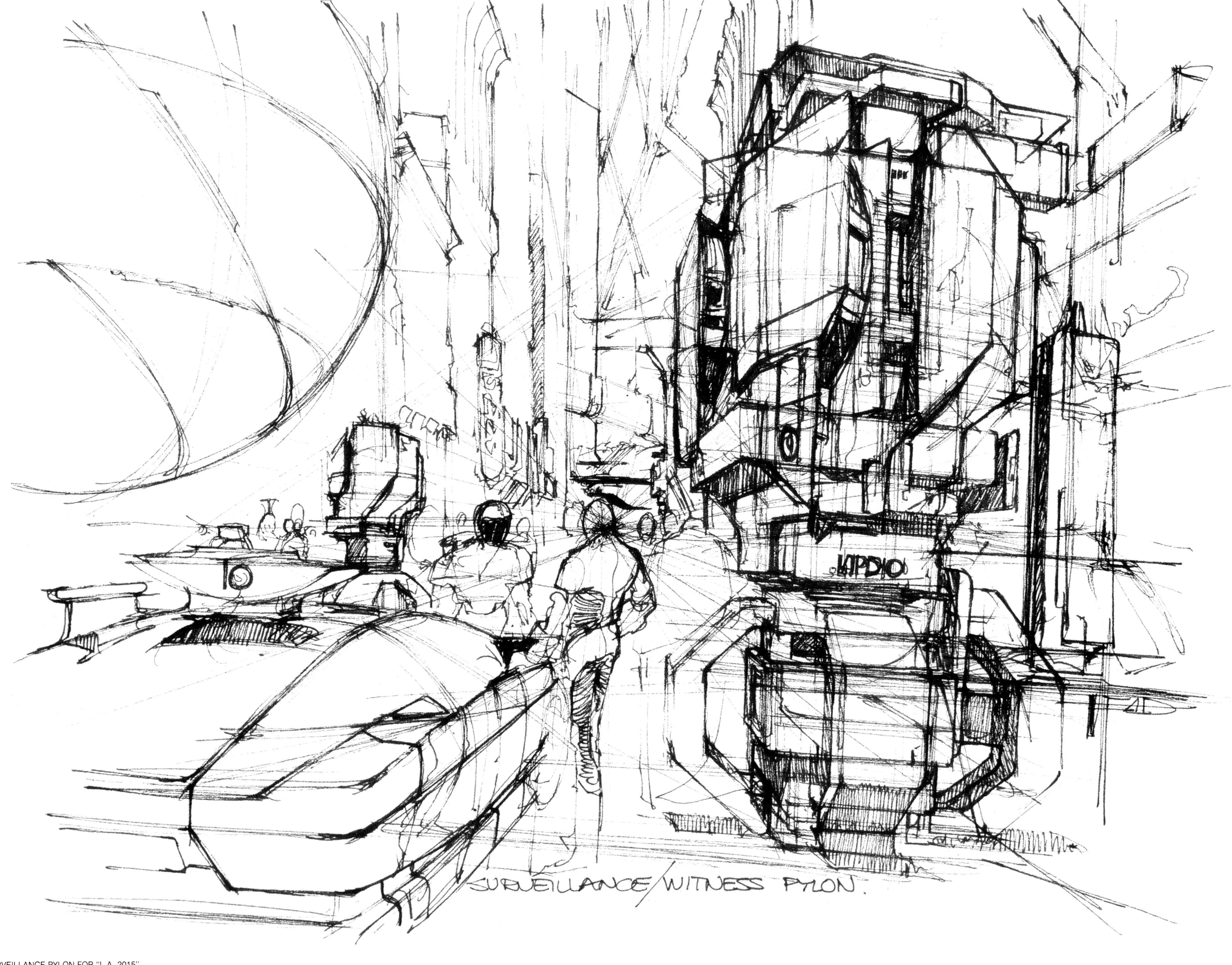

SURVEILLANCE/WITNESS PYLON.
LAPD101

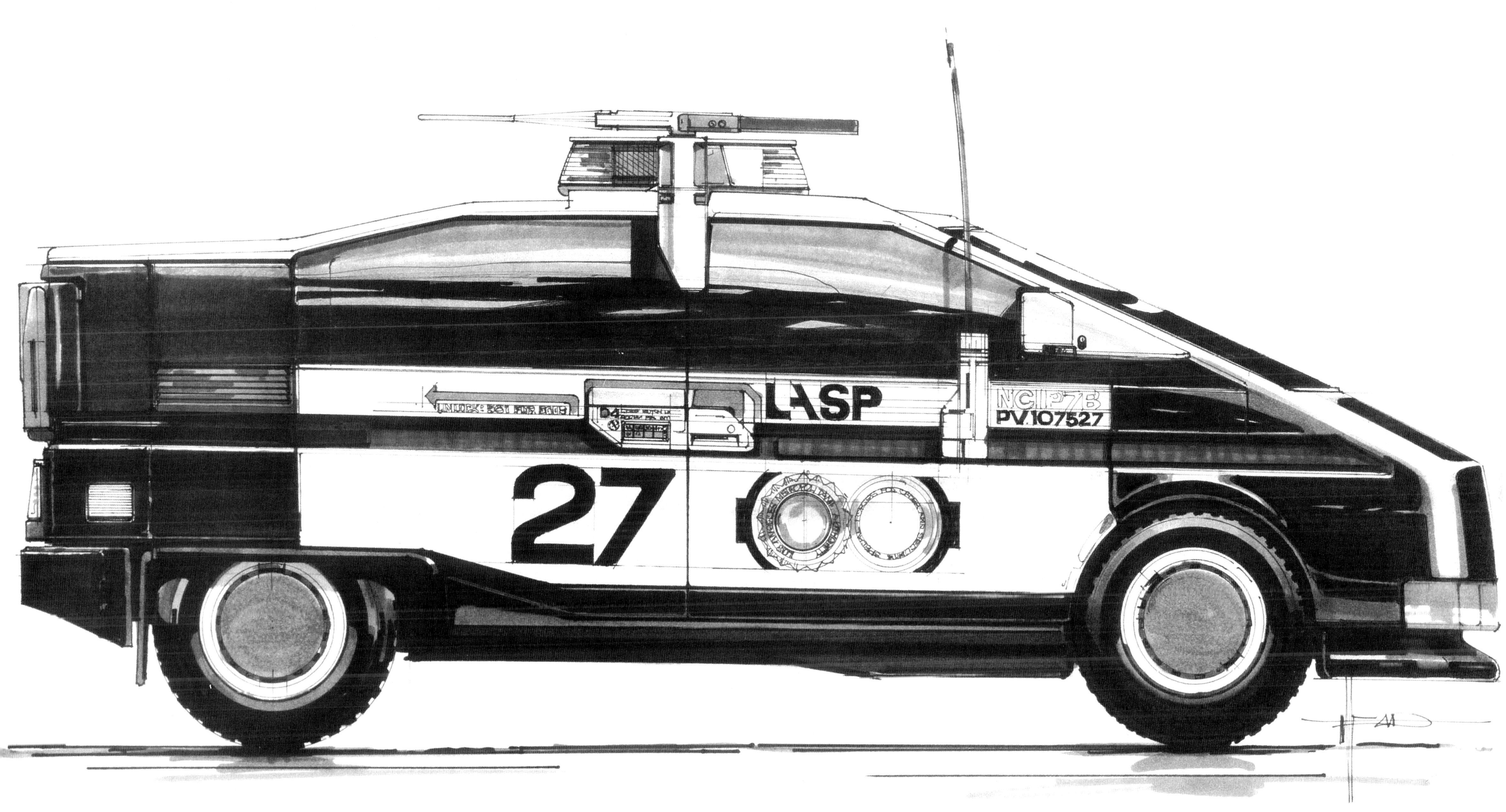

LASP
27
NCIP76
PV.107527

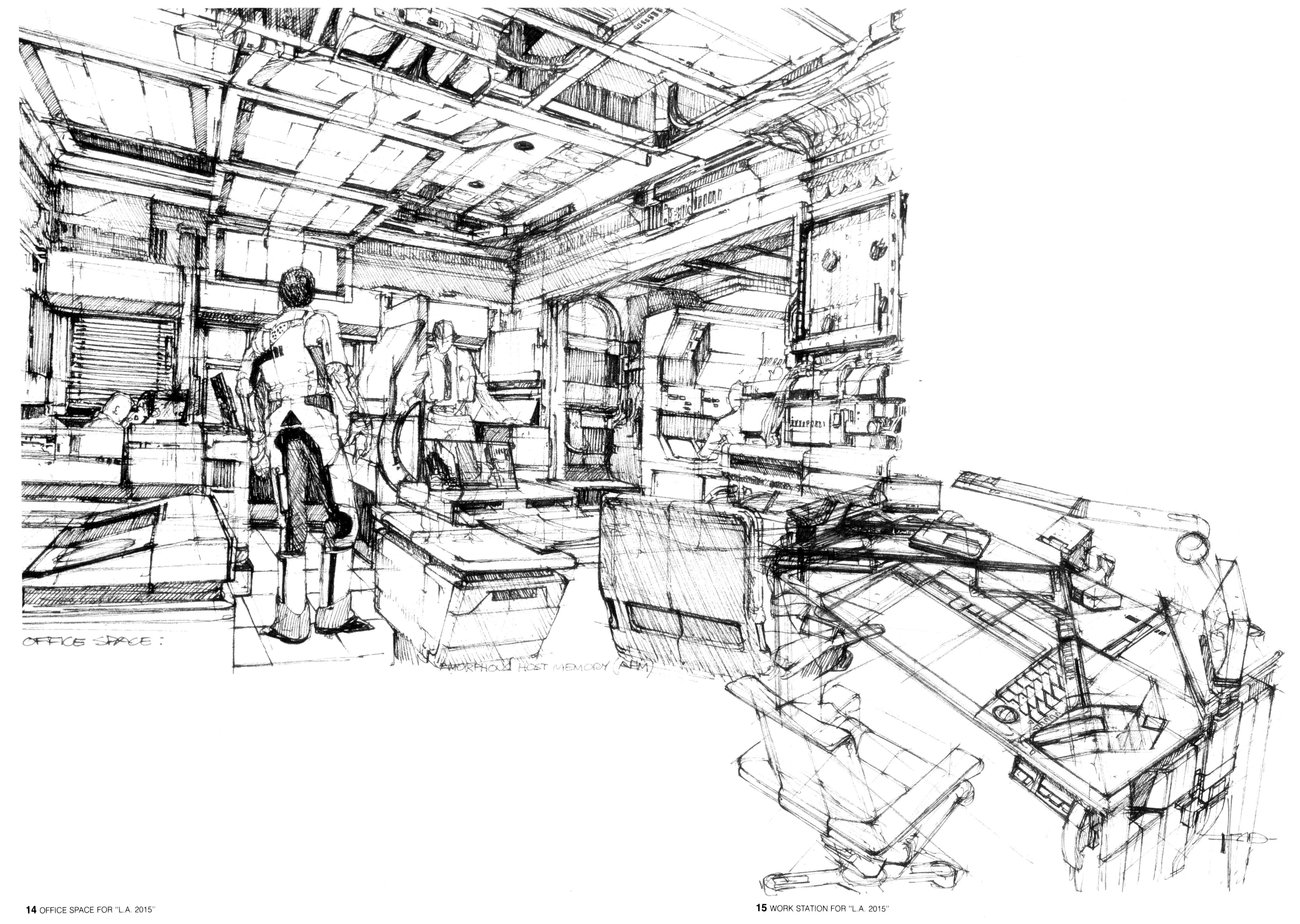

OFFICE SPACE:
AMORPHOUS HOST MEMORY (AHM)

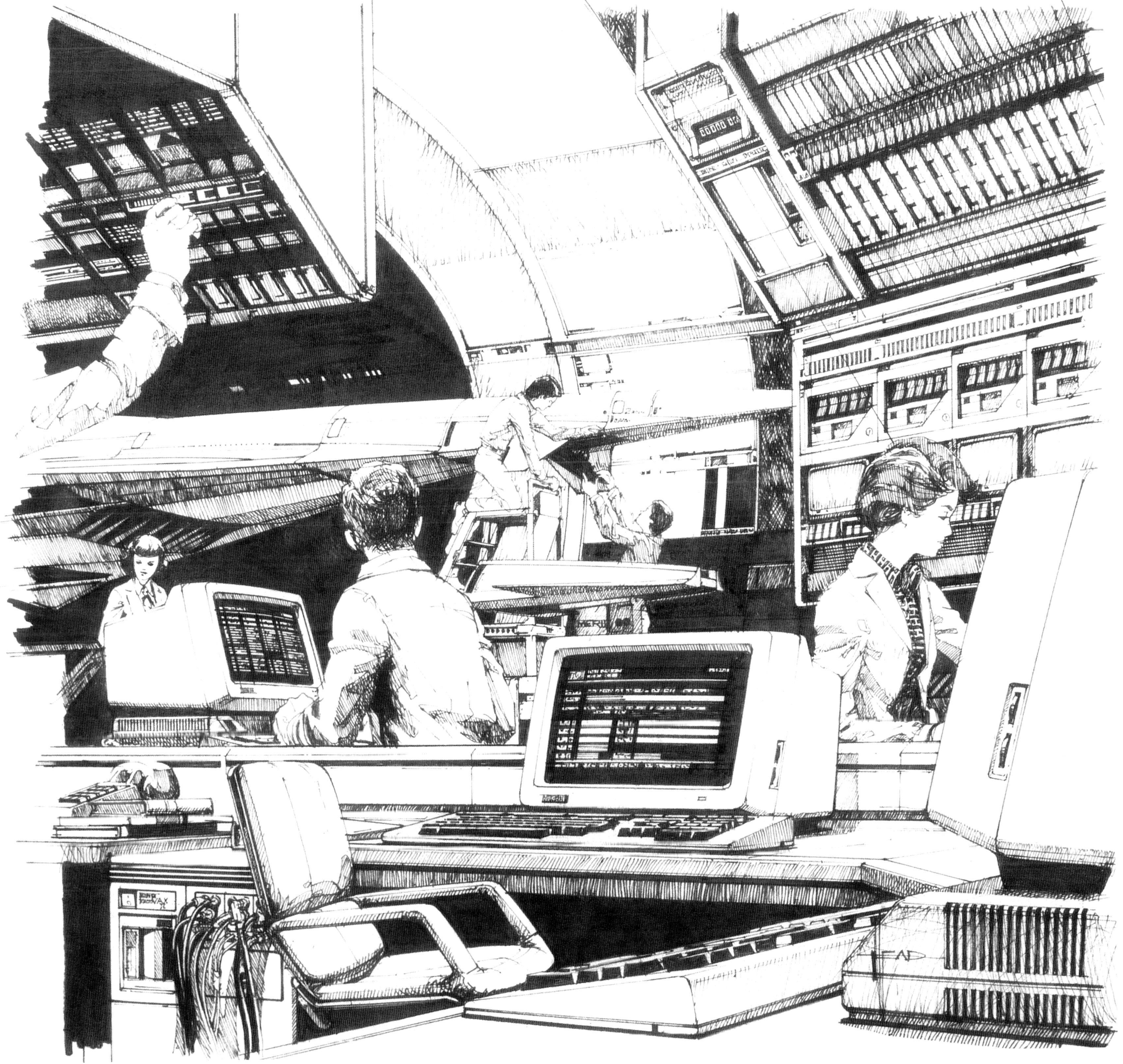

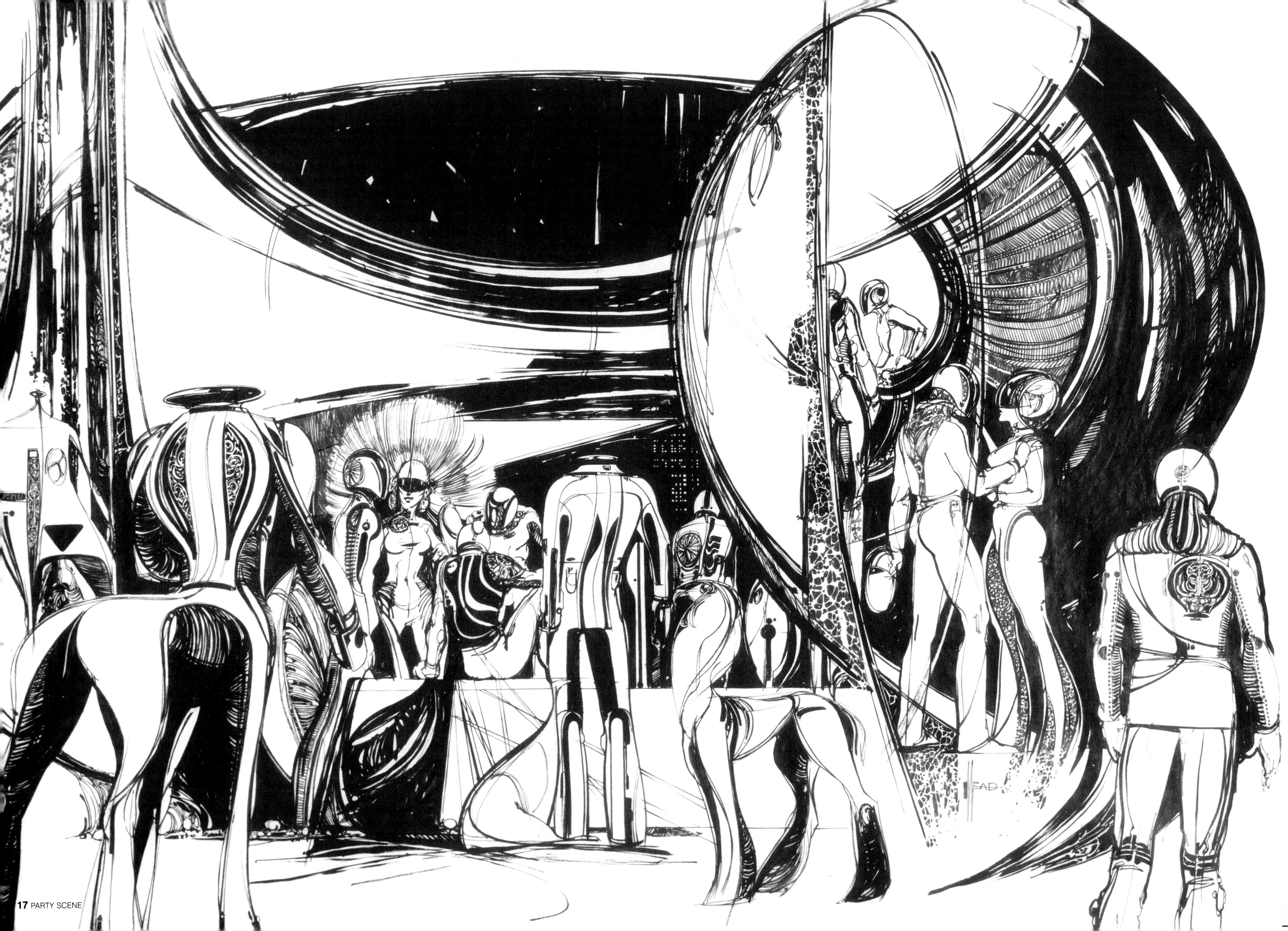

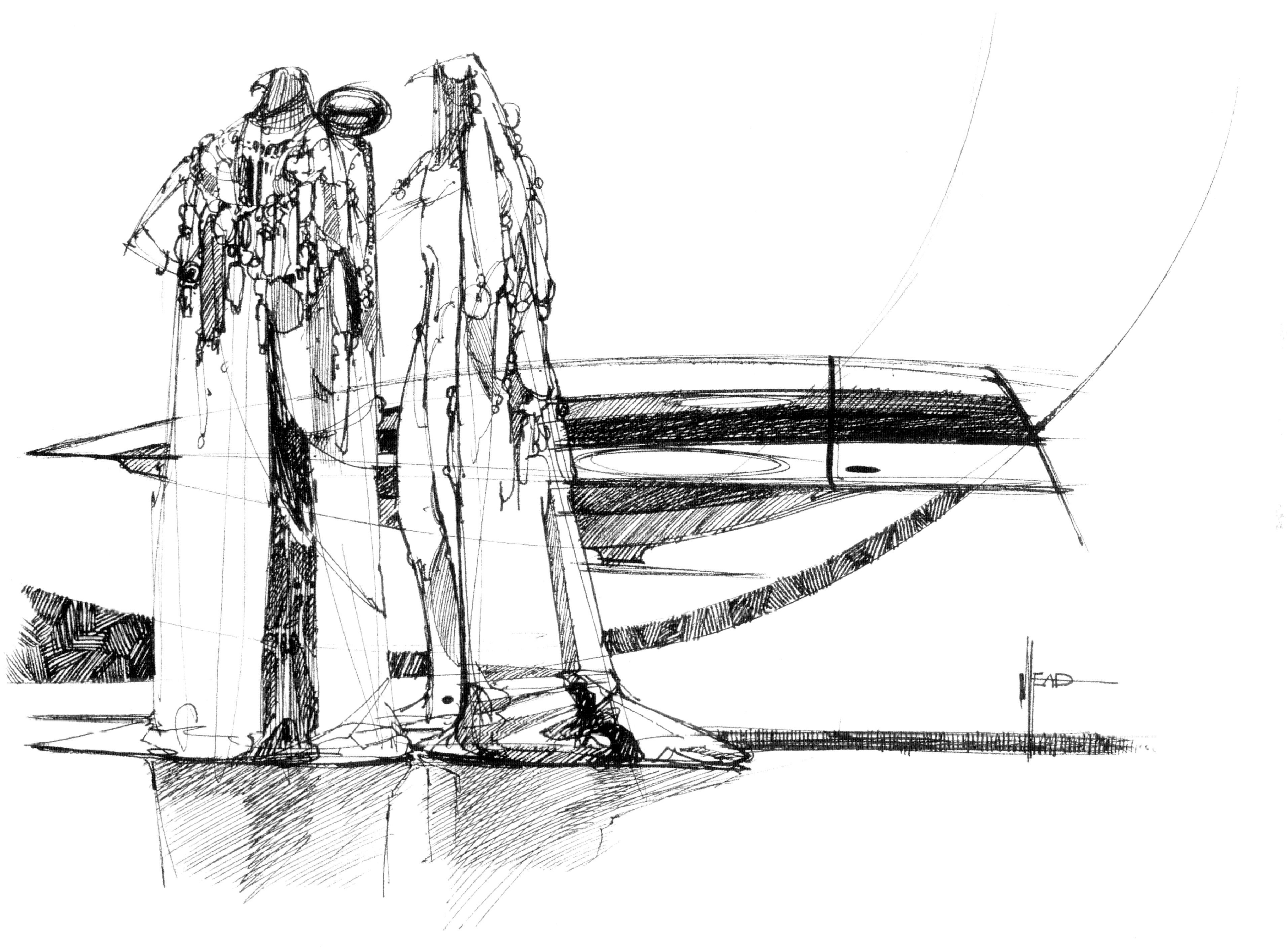

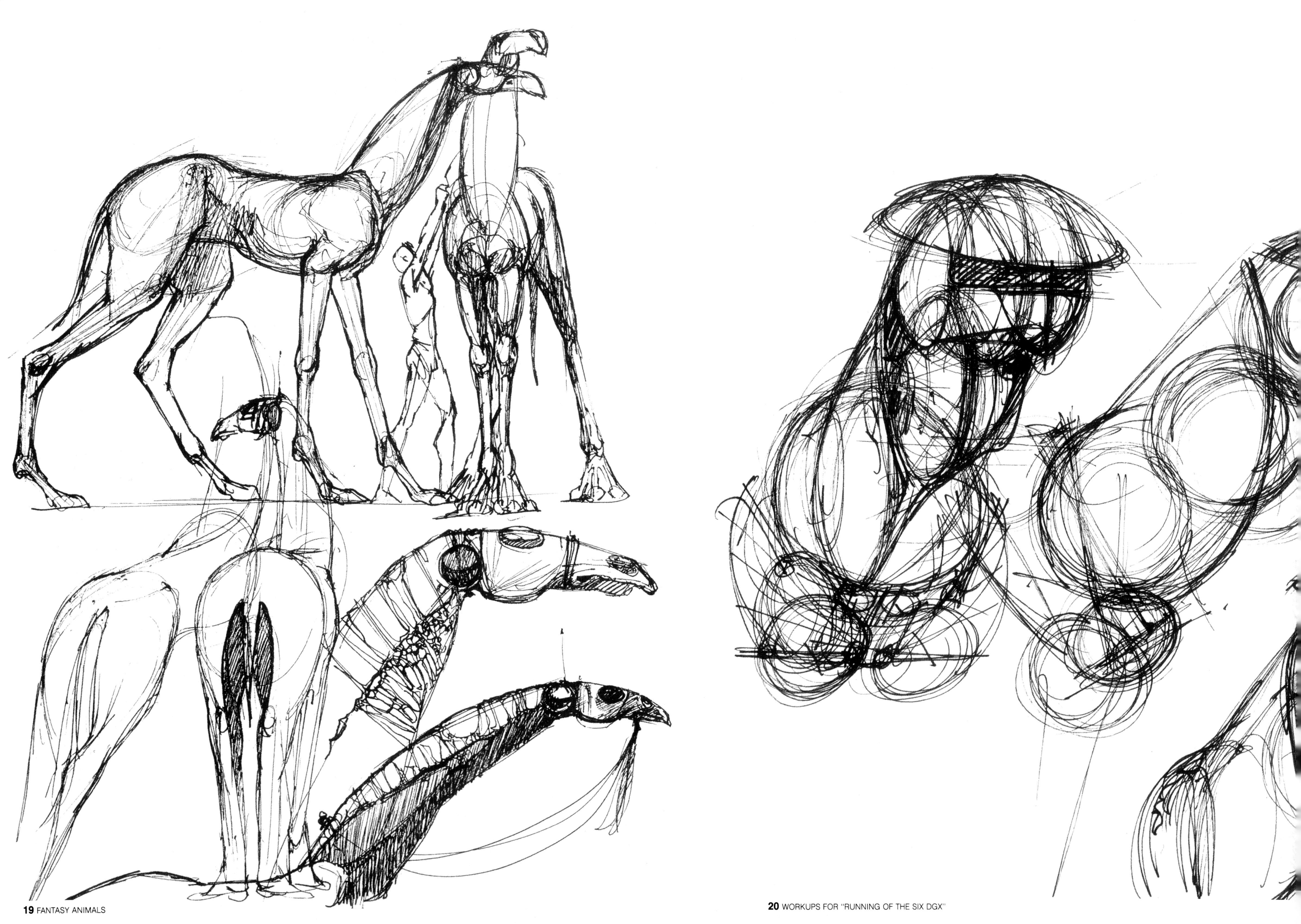

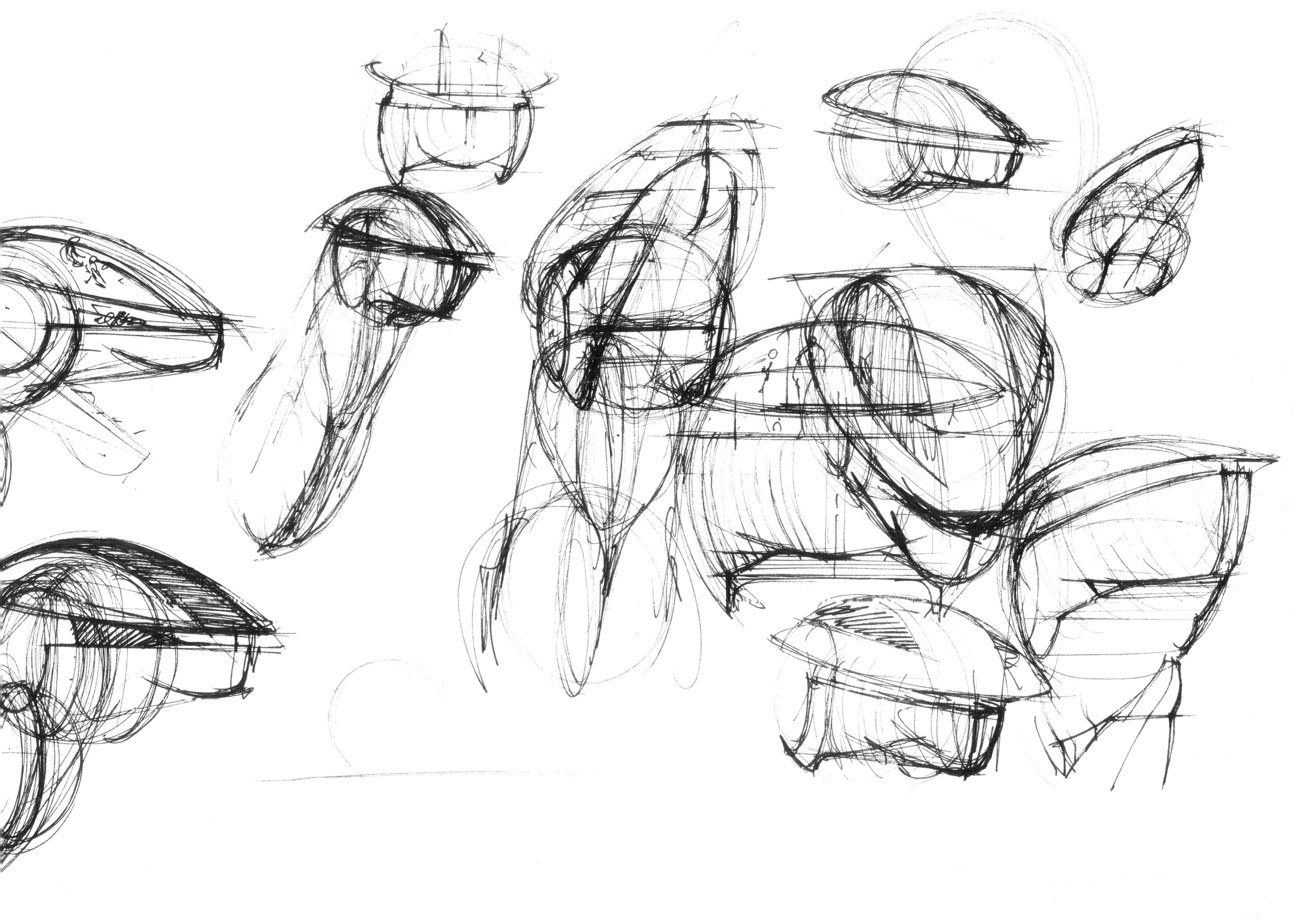

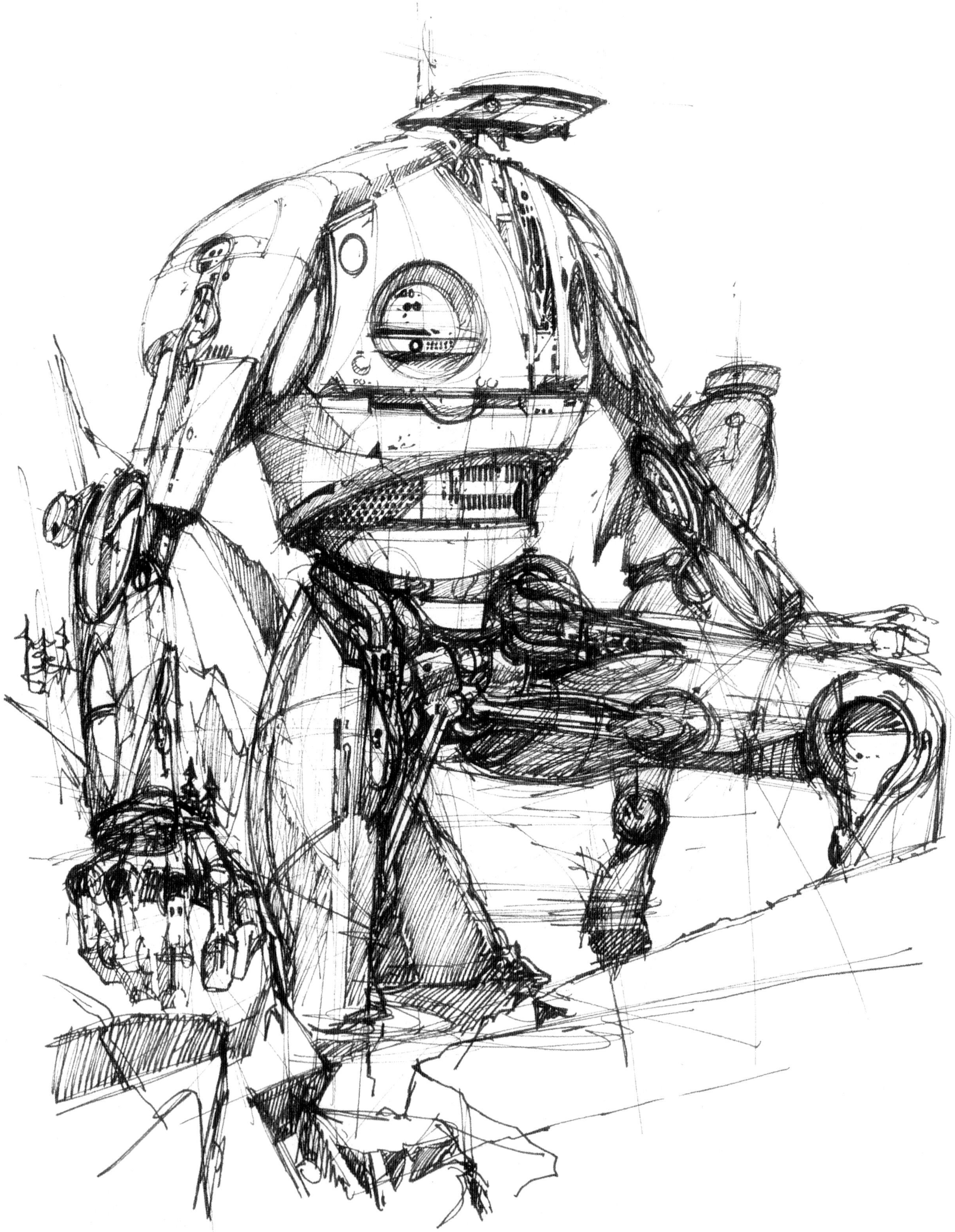

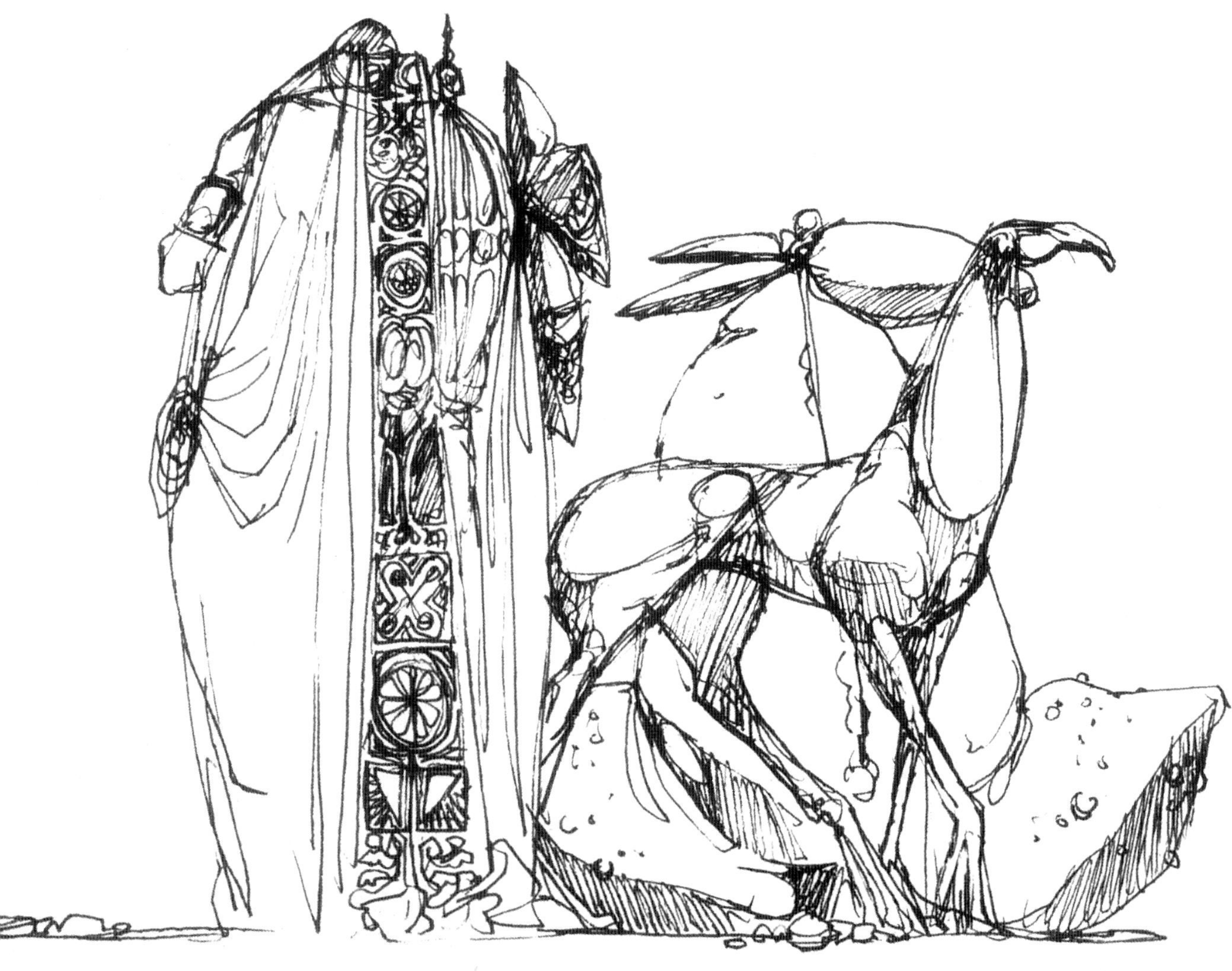

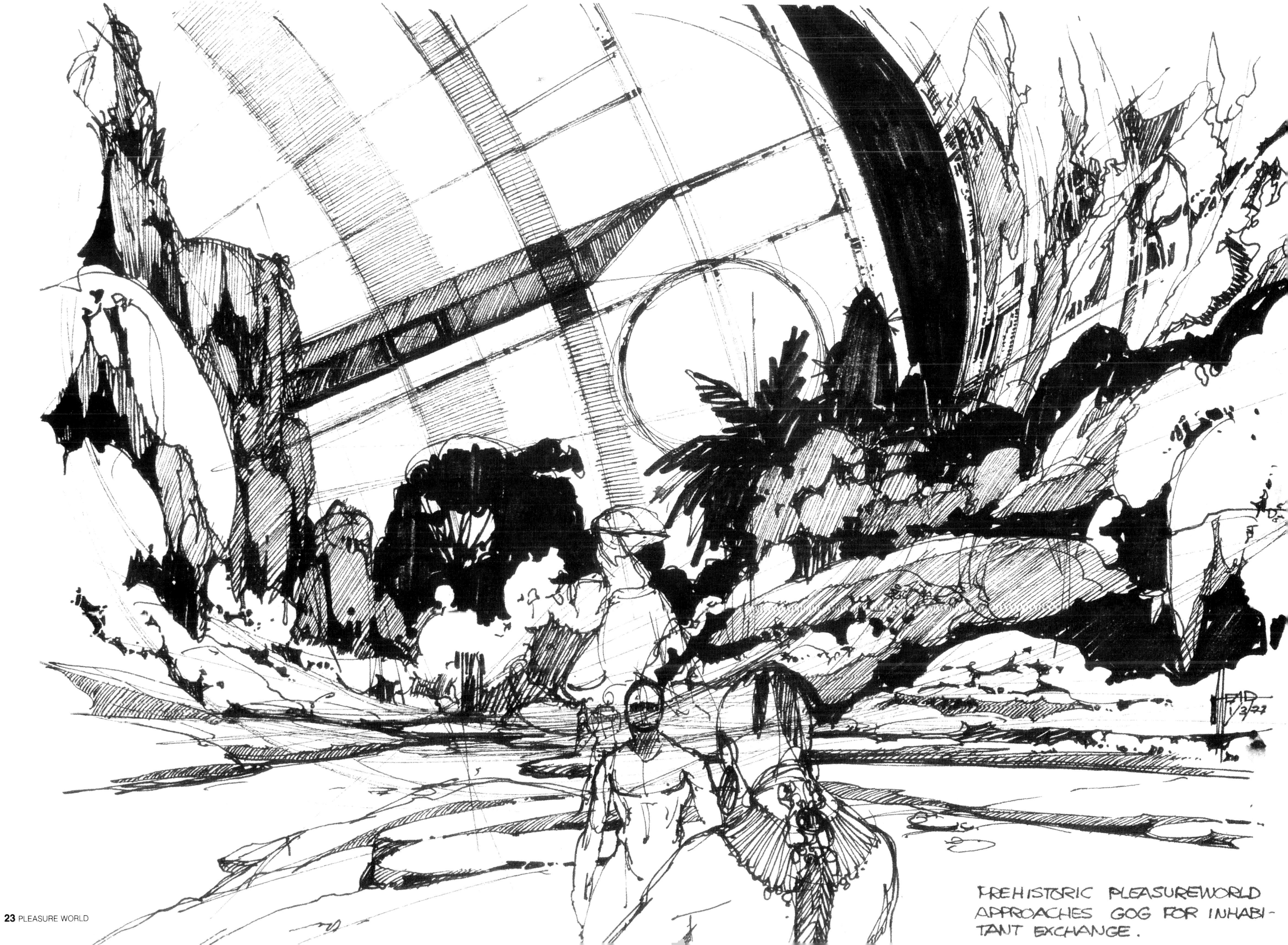

PREHISTORIC PLEASUREWORLD
APPROACHES GOG FOR INHABI-
TANT EXCHANGE.

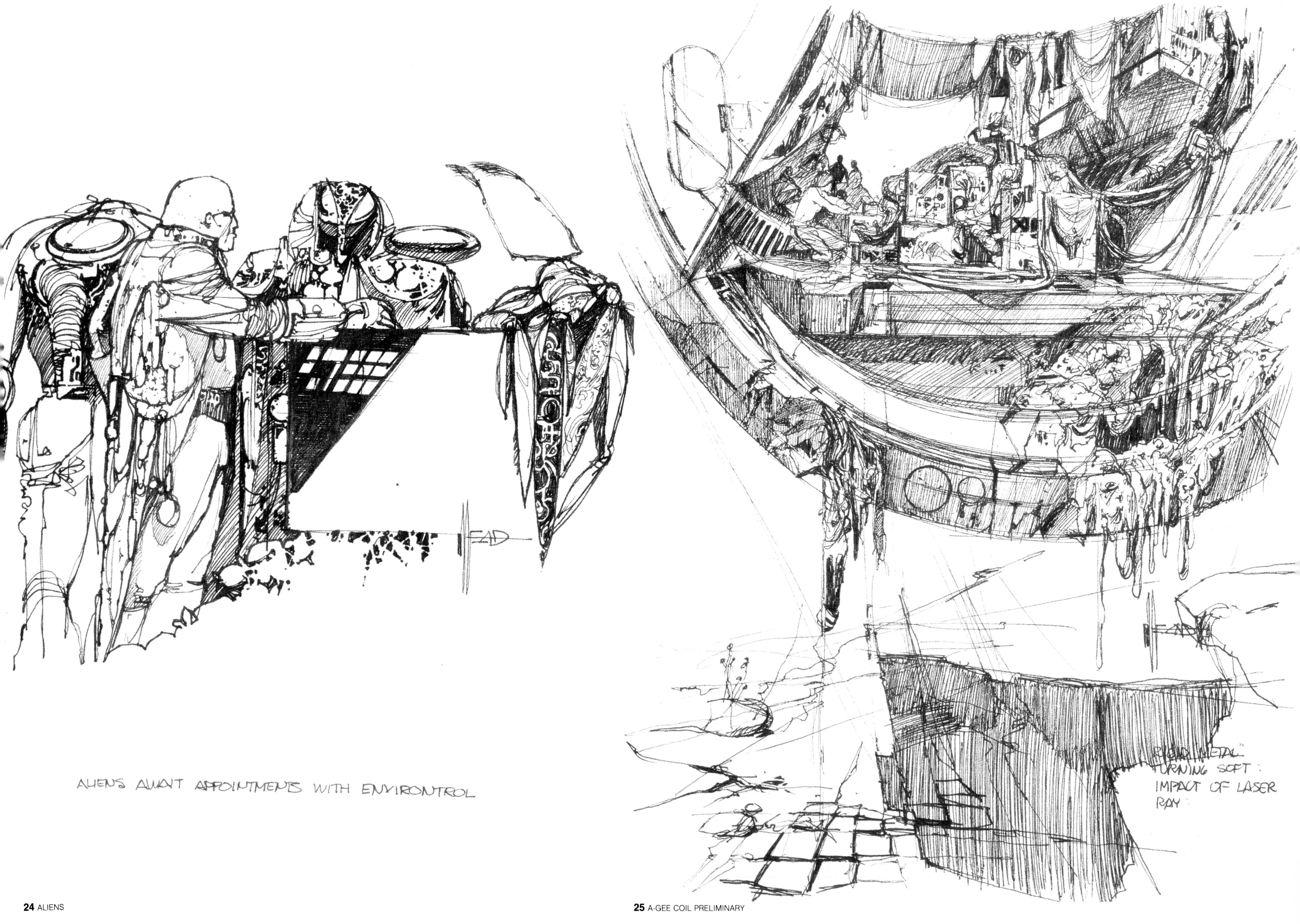

ALIENS AWAIT APPOINTMENTS WITH ENVIRONTROL
HARD METAL
TURNING SOFT:
IMPACT OF LASER
RAY

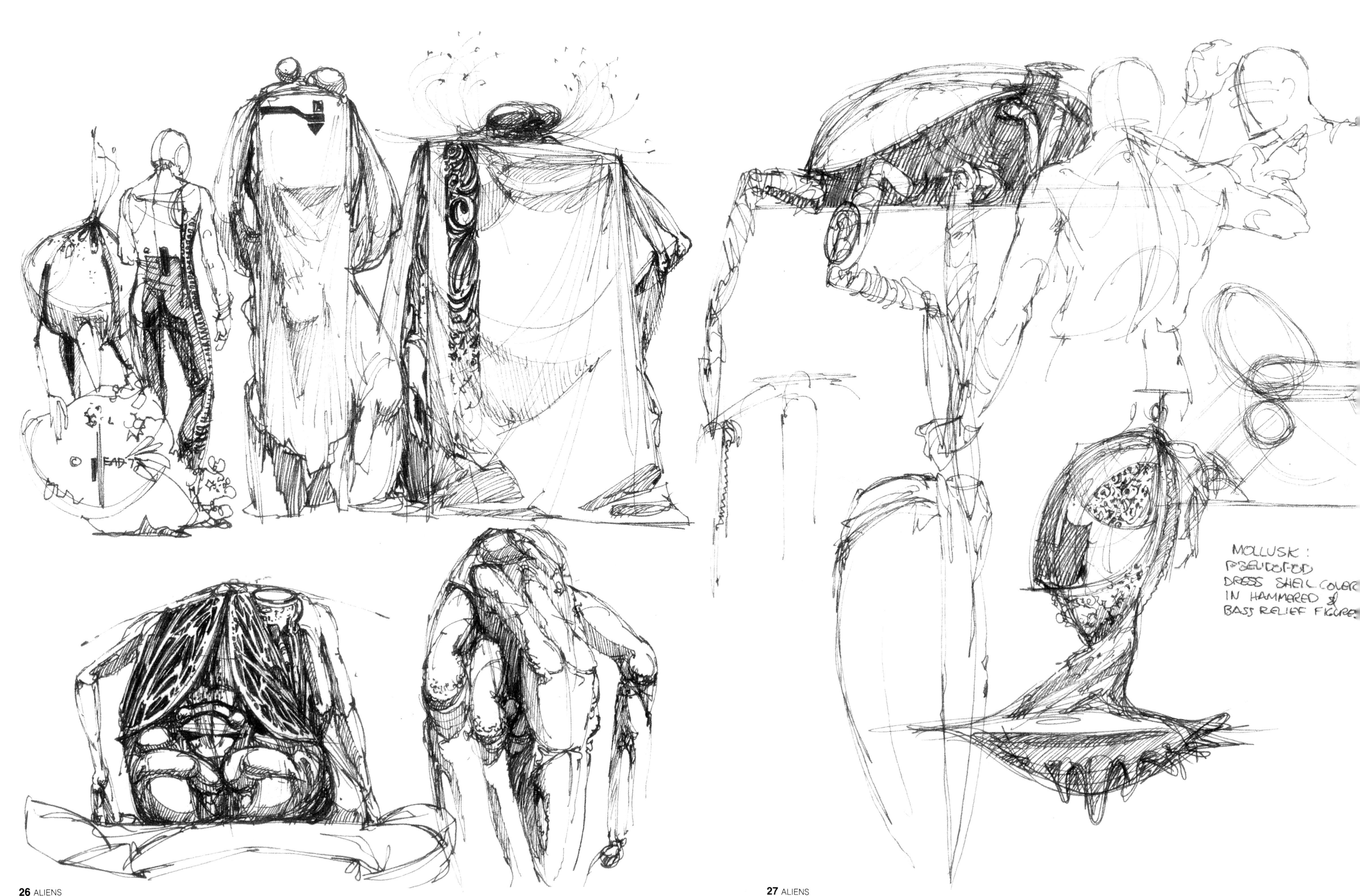

MOLLUSK:
PSEUDOPOD
DRESS SHELL COVER
IN HAMMERED &
BASS RELIEF FIGURES

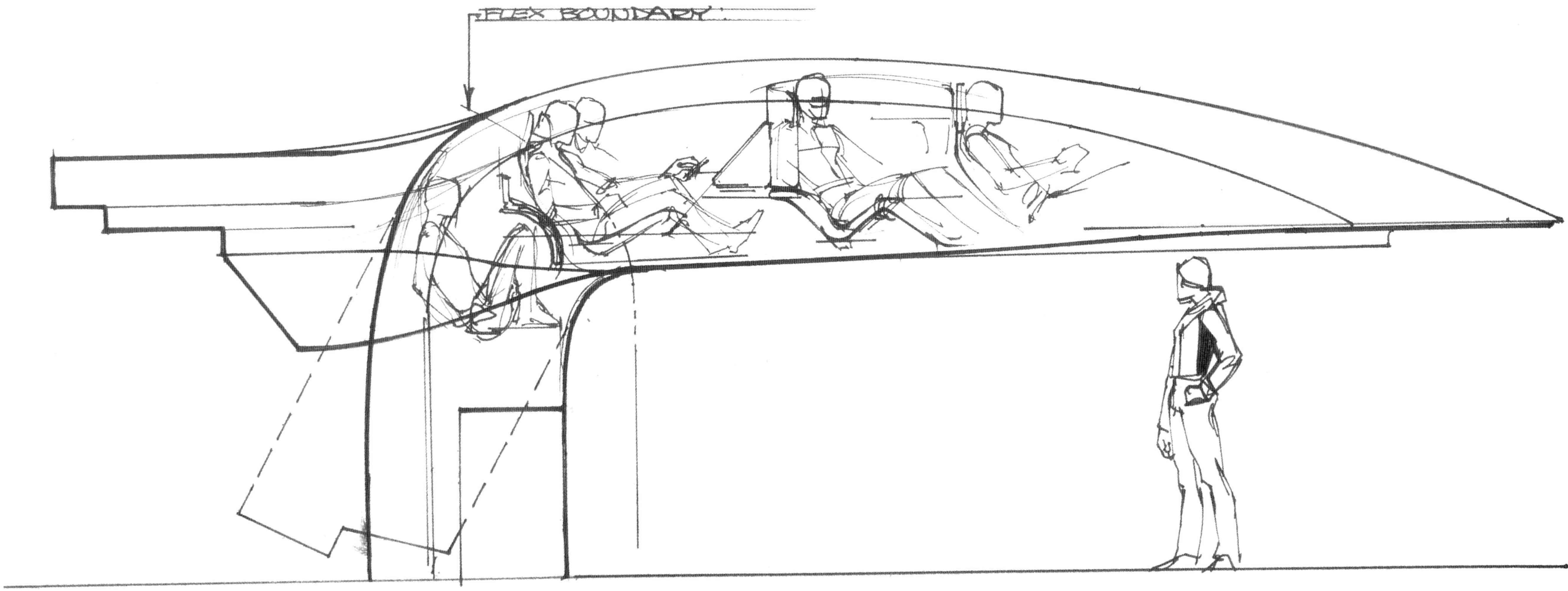

FLEX BOUNDARY

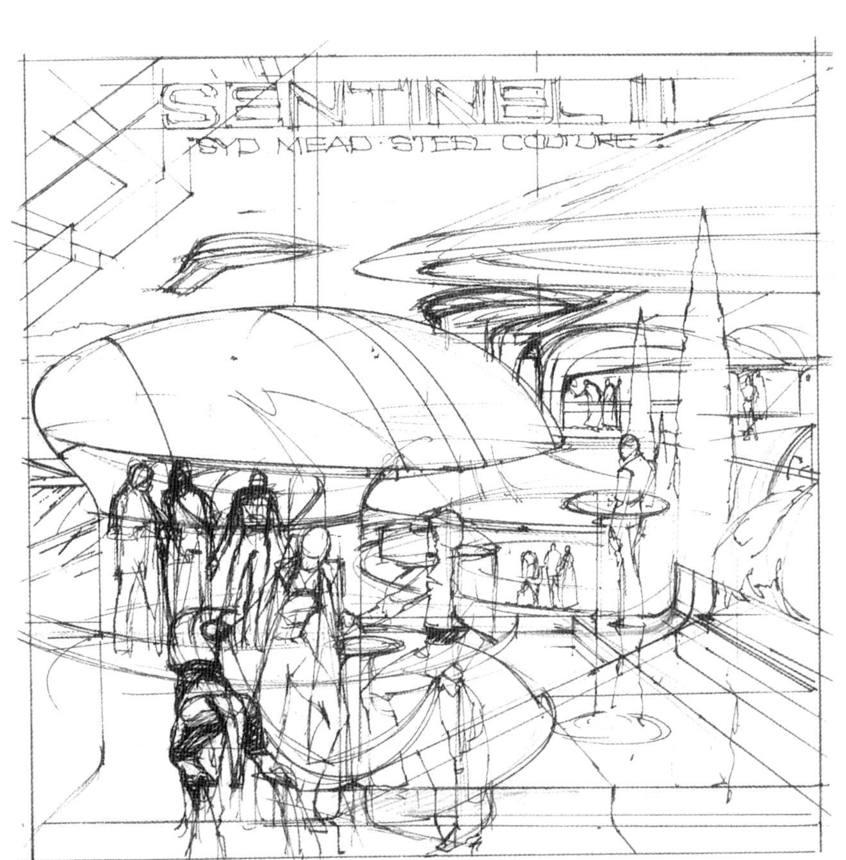

SENTINEL II
SYD MEAD · STEEL COUTURE

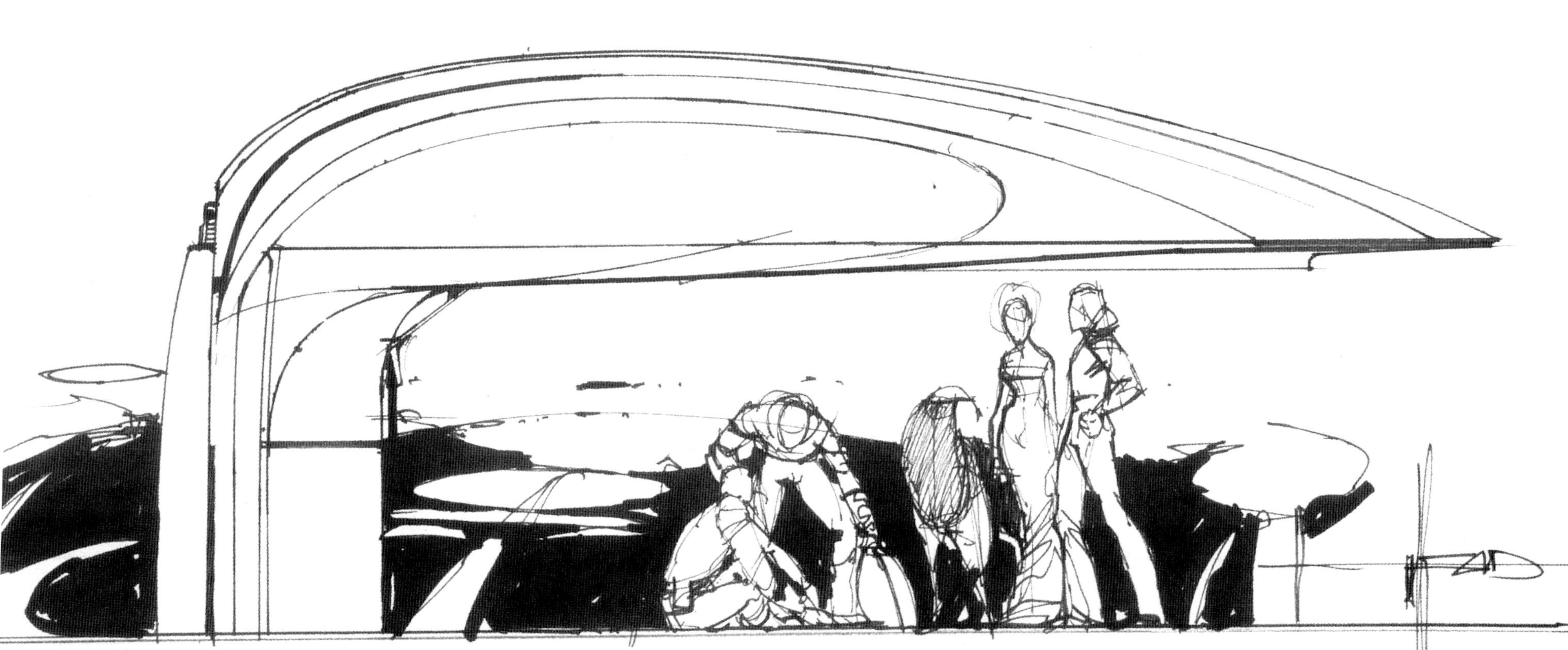

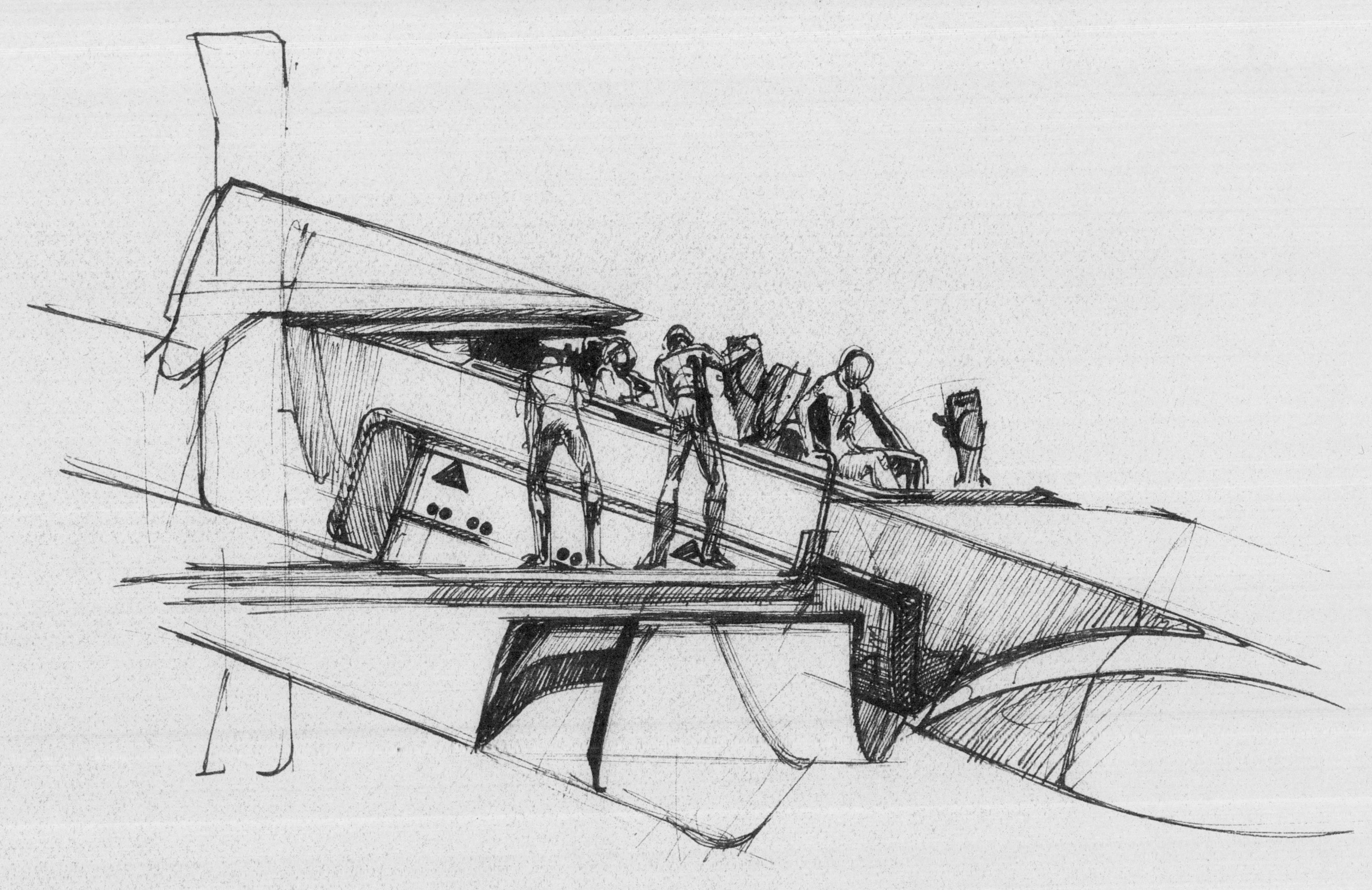

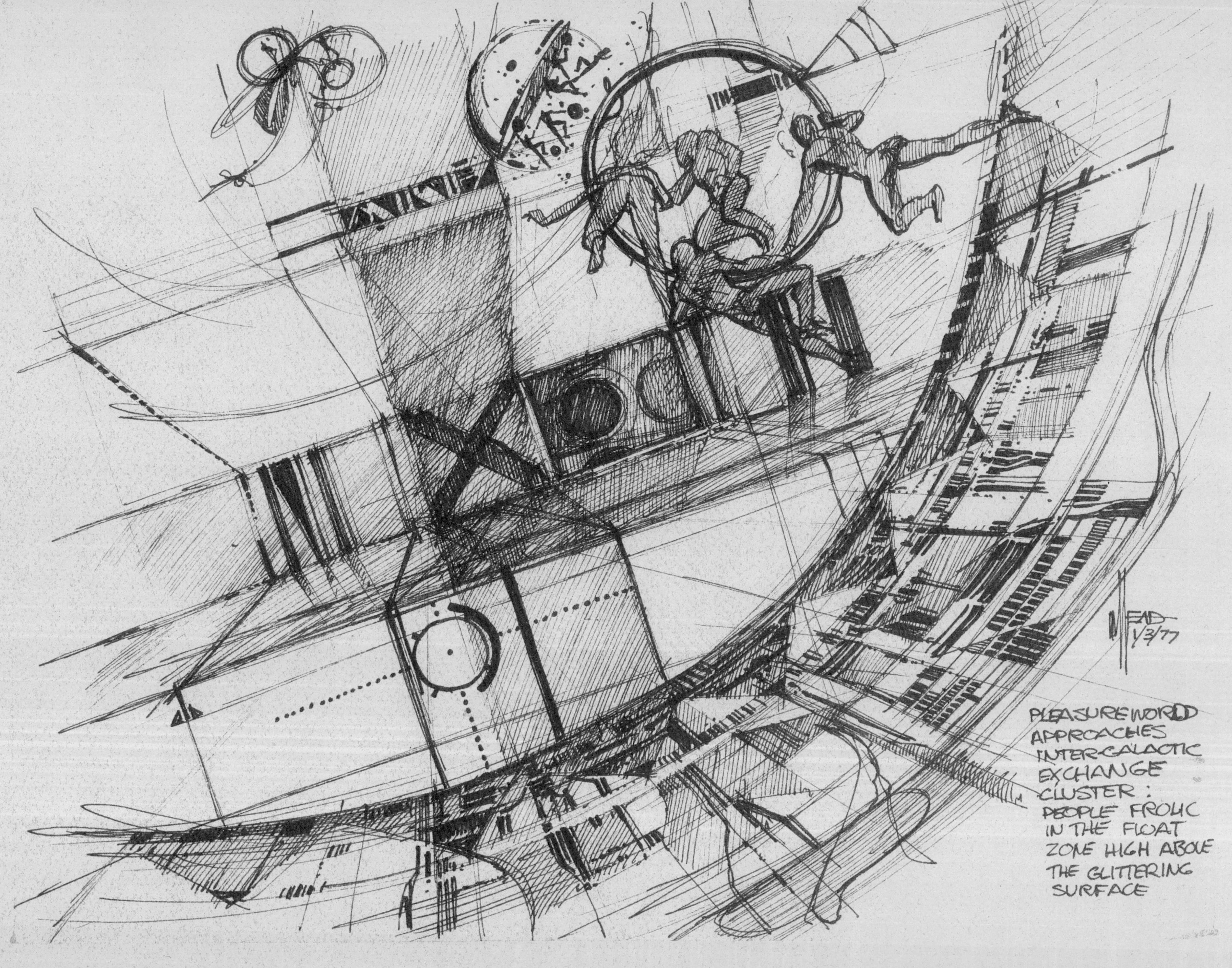

MEAD 1/3/77
PLEASURE WORLD
APPROACHES
INTERGALACTIC
EXCHANGE
CLUSTER:
PEOPLE FROLIC
IN THE FLOAT
ZONE HIGH ABOVE
THE GLITTERING
SURFACE

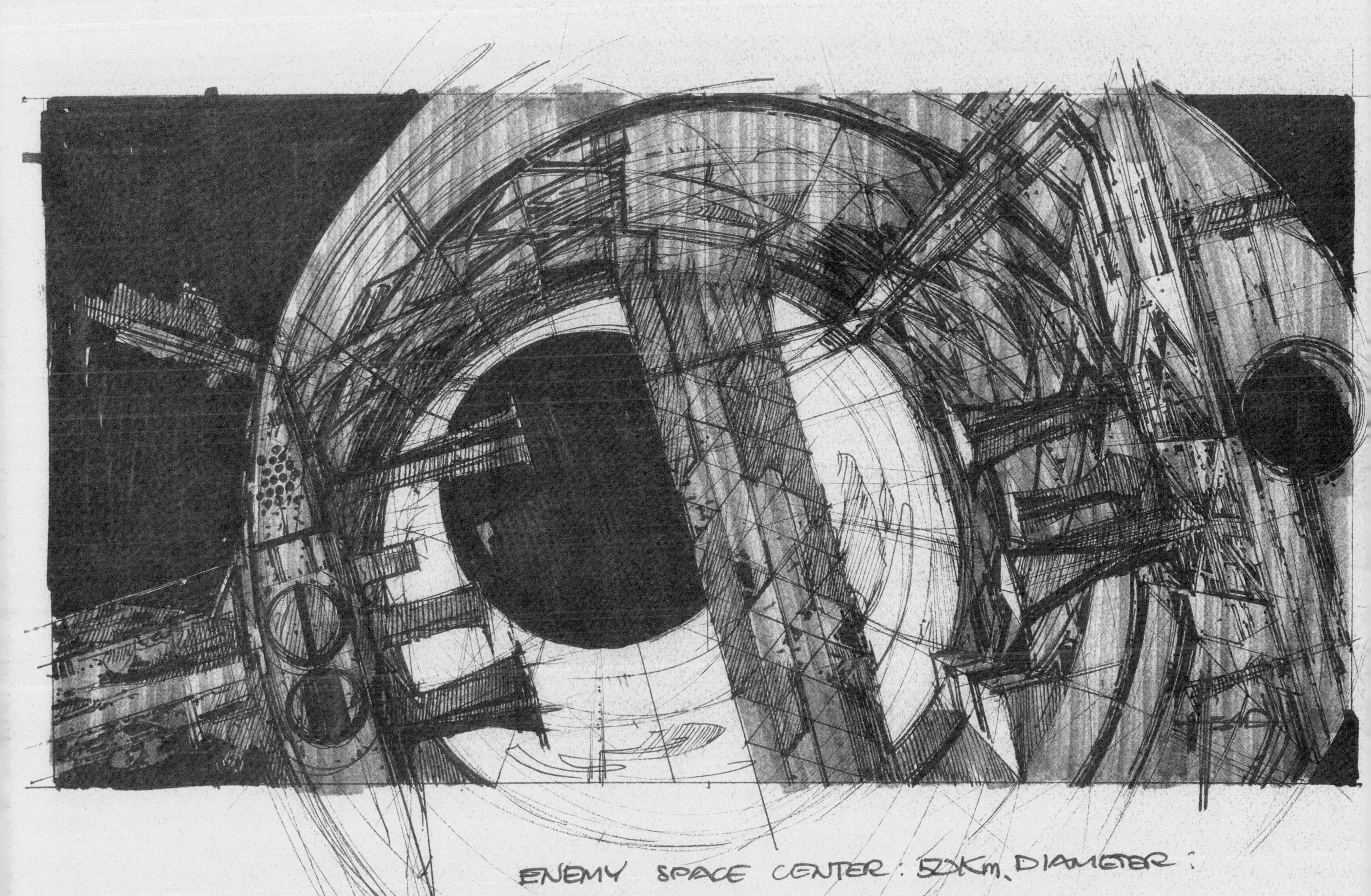

ENEMY SPACE CENTER : 52Km. DIAMETER :

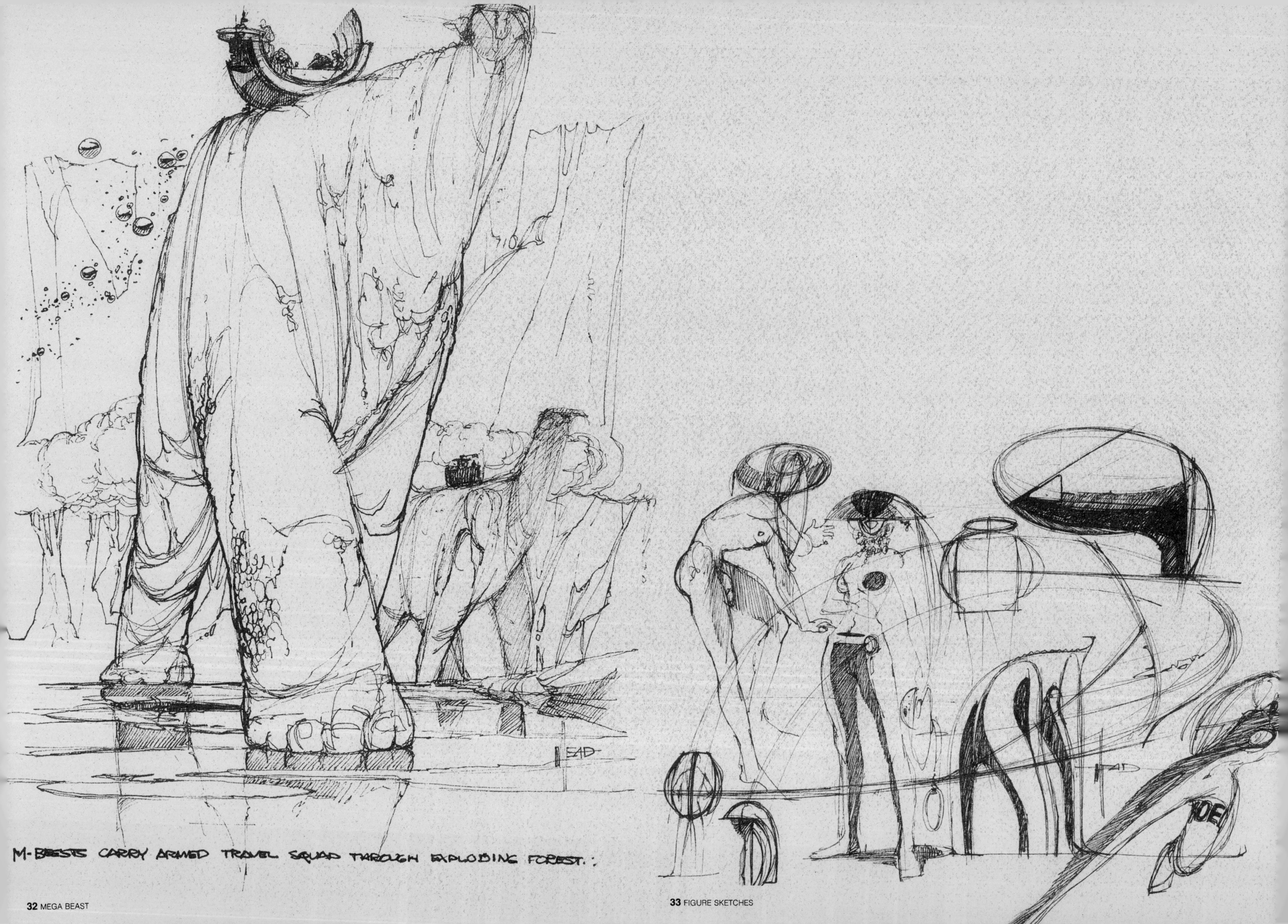
M-BEASTS CARRY ARMED TRAVEL SQUAD THROUGH EXPLODING FOREST.

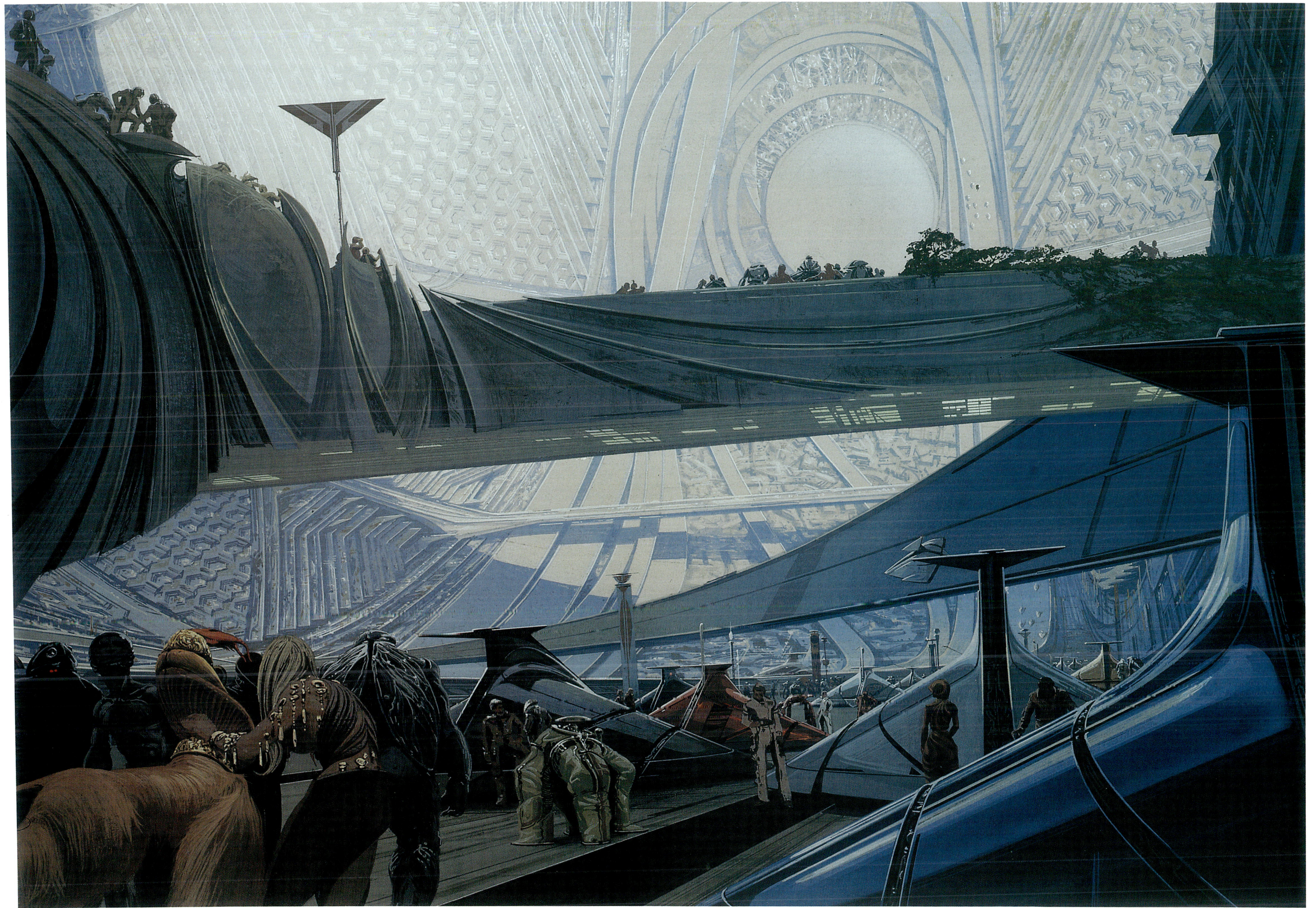

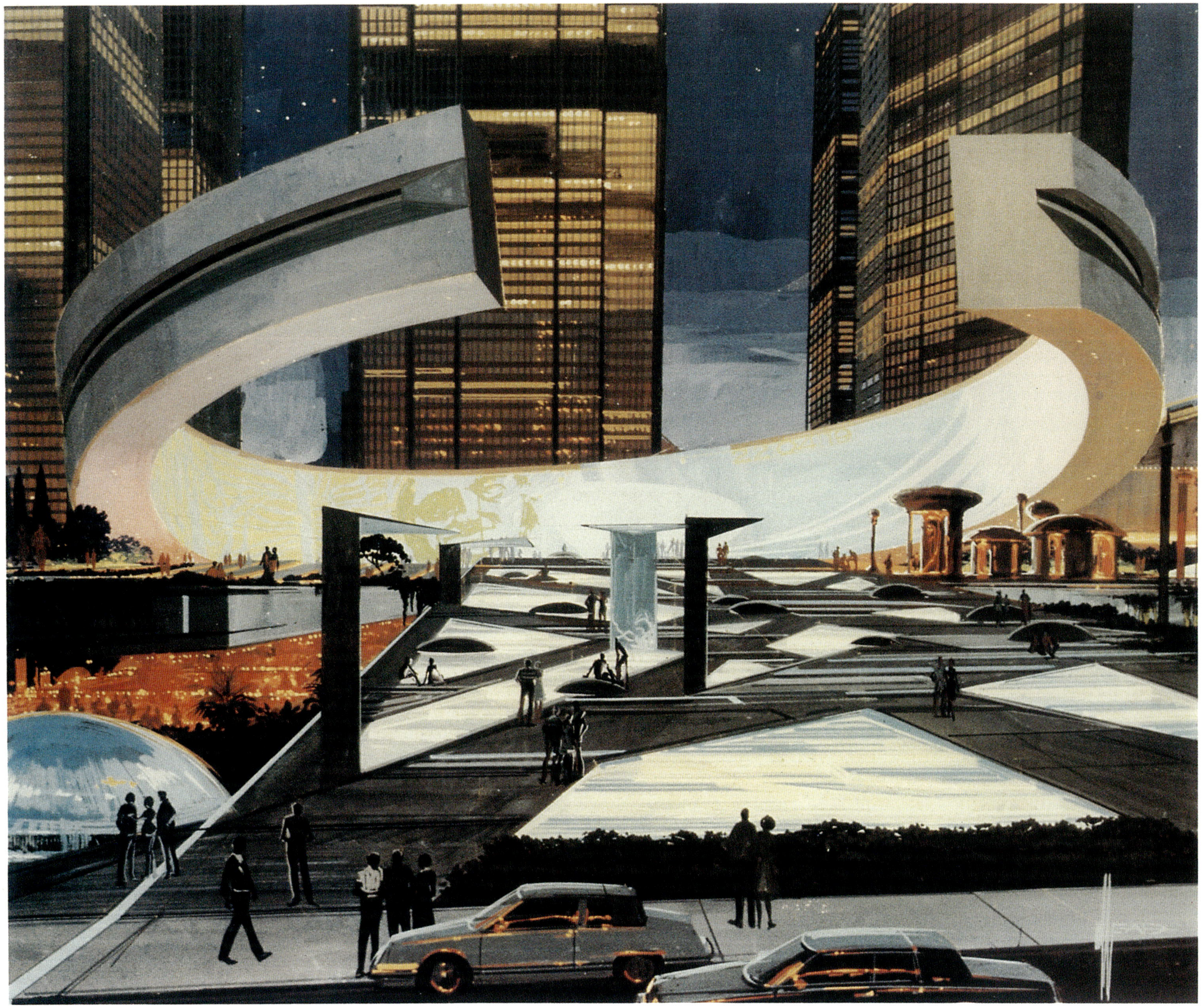

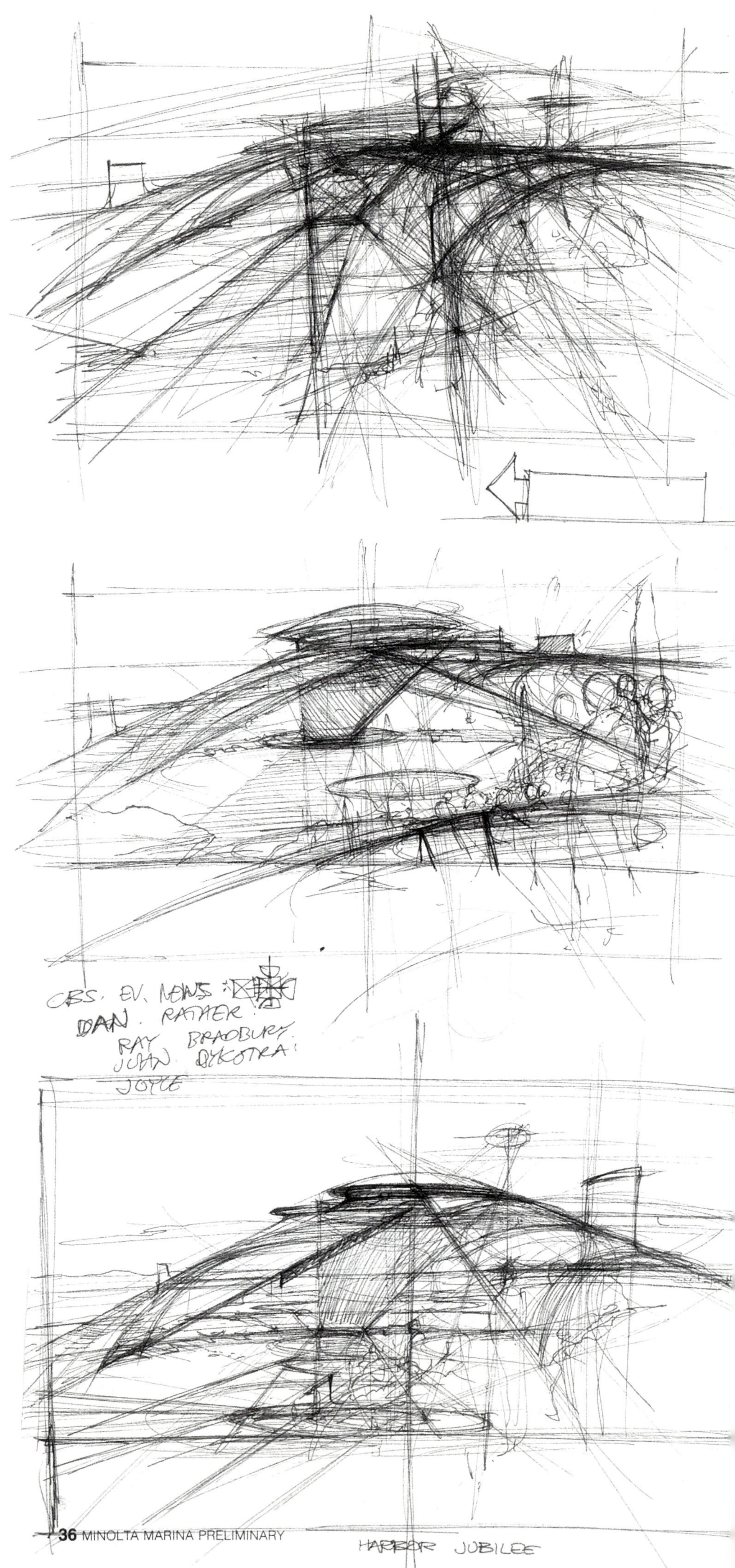
CBS. EV. NEWS
DAN. RATHER
RAY BRADBURY
JOHN DYKSTRA
JOYCE
HARBOR JUBILEE

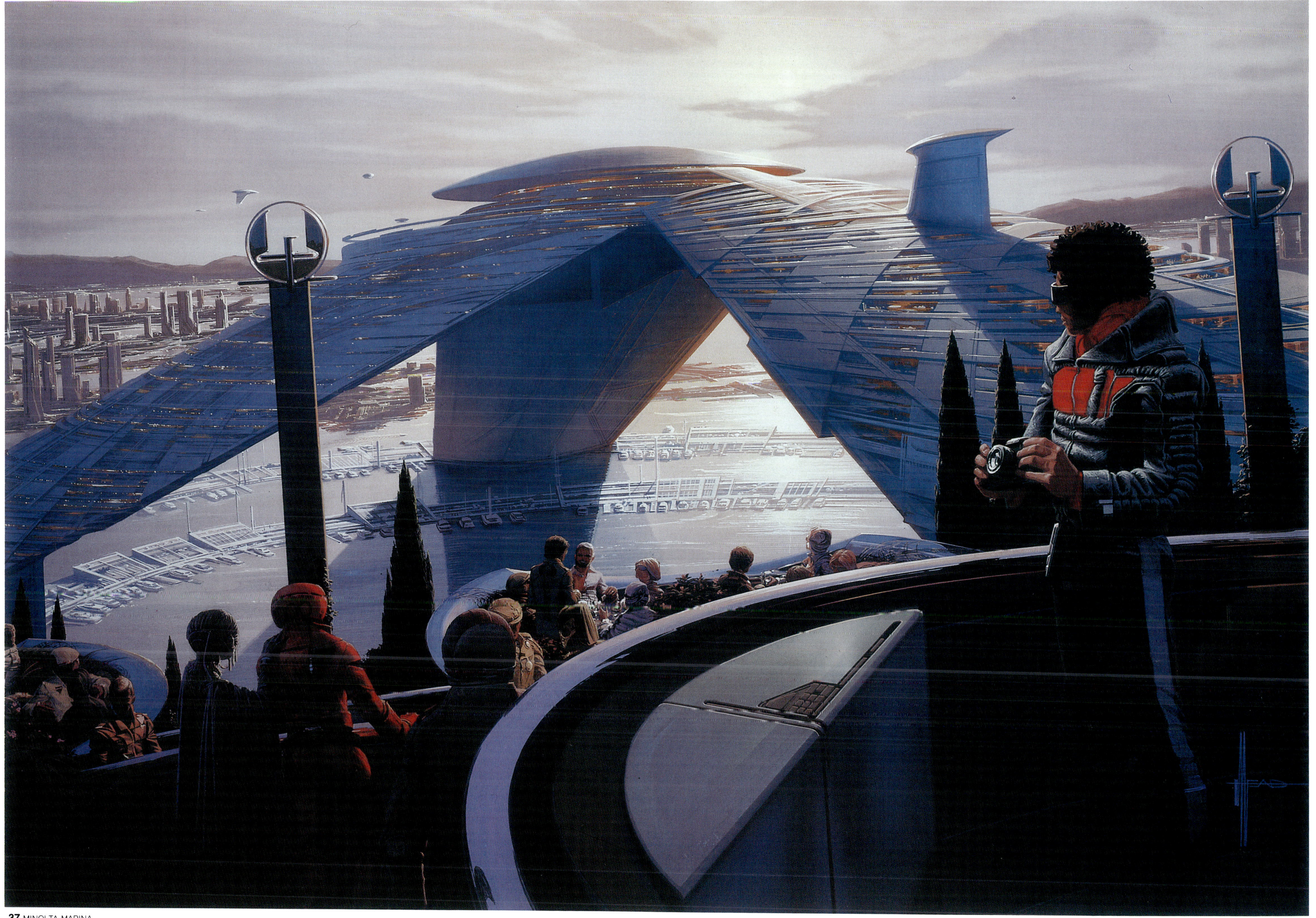

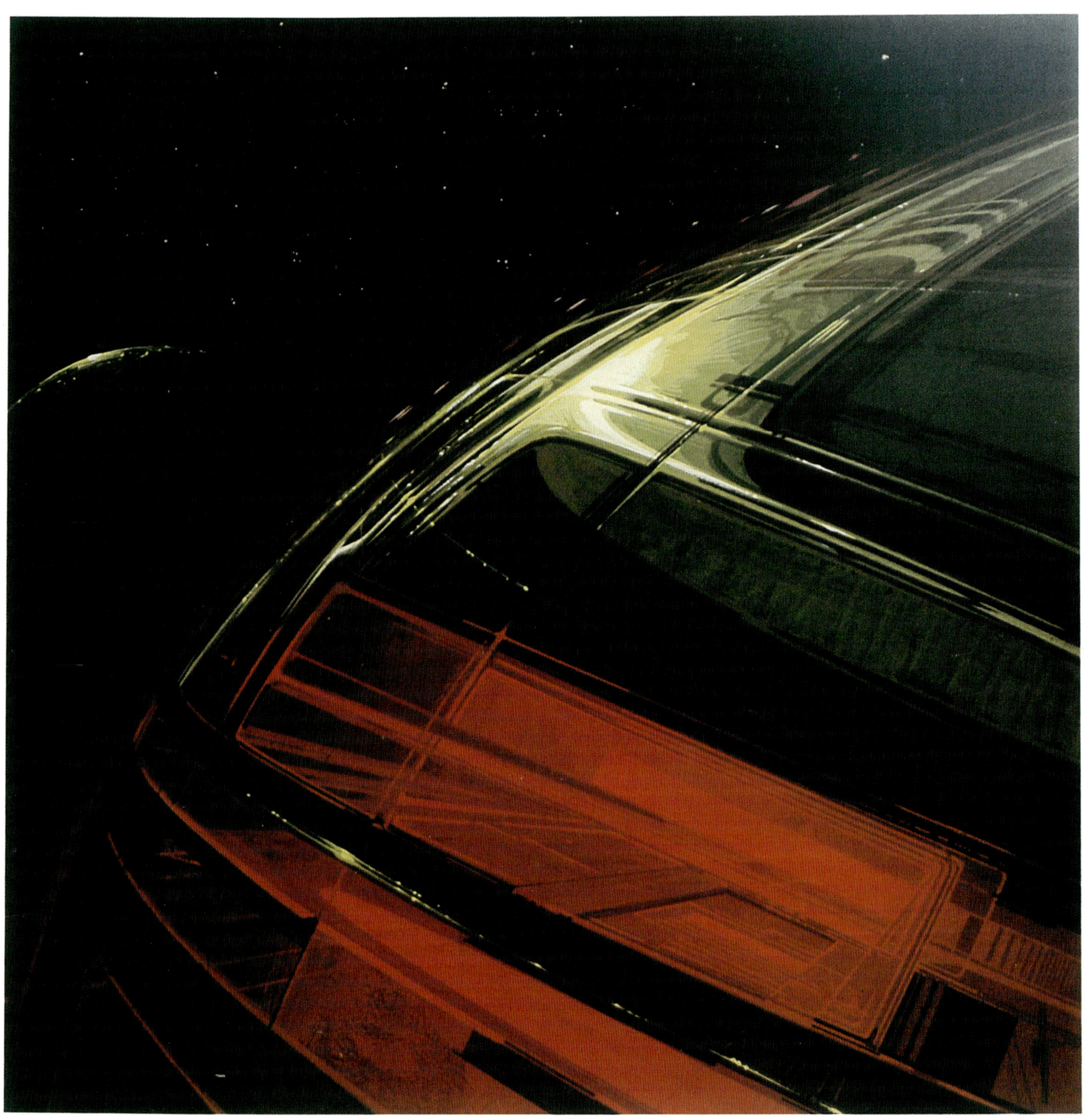

Originally published as

"STUDIO IMAGE ONE"

Published By OBLAGON, INC.

OBLAGON Inc.
728 Burleigh Drive
Pasadena, CA 91105
Phone (626) 441-3737
www.SYDMEAD.com

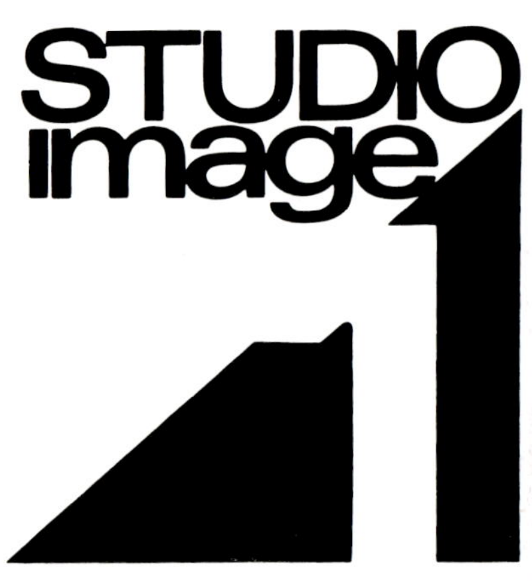

COMMISSIONING ENTITIES FOR THE FOLLOWING WORKS:

1. Yurakucho Seibu Co., Ltd.

2. 3. Rays Co., Ltd.

4. 5. 6. 7. 8. Jey Dey

9. 10. 11. 12. 13. 14. 15. Peter Hyams Productions, Inc.

© WARNER BROS.

16. Digital Corporation

17. Automobile Quarterly

20. 34. Dela Corporation, Inc.

35. Texas Eastern Transmission

36. 37. Minolta Corporation

38. Opel Dealer Association

PRODUCTION CREDIT
All Illustrations: Syd Mead
Executive Producer: Peter Schneider
Associate Producer: Mieko Ichikawa
Art Direction: Michael Hughes
Photography: Michael Hughes
Layout Design: Syd Mead, Inc.

Published August 1988
Printed by Dai Nippon in Japan

ISBN-0-929463-00-5

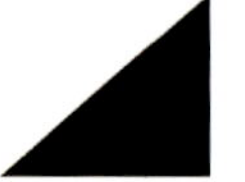

**Reissue by Design Studio Press
March, 2024
Printed in China, 978-1-624650-78-9**